Ephesians 5
Romance
the Truth about Love

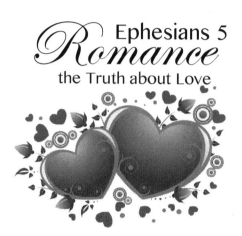

Dr. Debi Smith

Dream Dance Books
Newport Beach, California

Ephesians 5 Romance:
the Truth about Love
by Dr. Debi Smith

For information write to:
      Dr. Debi Smith
      Orange County Christian Counseling, Inc.
      PO Box 13154
      Newport Beach, CA 92658
      www.DrDebiSmith.com

ISBN: 978-0-9885934-4-2

Printed in the United States of America

Dedicated to My Beloved

*I belong to my beloved;
and his desire is for me.*
~ Song of Solomon 7:10

ACKNOWLEDGEMENTS 7

Part 1: Your Love Story Matters

A DELIGHTFUL INHERITANCE 11

CHAPTER 1: ONCE UPON A TIME 15

CHAPTER 2: HOW TO WRITE A LOVE STORY 21

Part 2: Our Father's Love Story

THE GARDEN OF EDEN 27

CHAPTER 3: IN THE BEGINNING 33

CHAPTER 4: FALLING FOR THE LIE 37

CHAPTER 5: LIVING UNDER THE CURSE 43

CHAPTER 6: HEAVEN COMES TO EARTH 47

CHAPTER 7: THE SPIRIT OF TRUTH ABIDES 53

Part 3: The Psychology of Relationships

THE STUDY OF ROMANCE 57

CHAPTER 8: YOUR LONGING FOR LOVE 61

CHAPTER 9: ATTACHED AND ATTUNED 65

CHAPTER 10: SIMPLE FACTS ABOUT MARRIAGE 73

CHAPTER 11: COUPLES ONLY HAVE ONE PROBLEM 77

Part 4: The Beauty of a Woman

UNDERSTANDING AND LOVE 83

CHAPTER 12: NOT SO COMPLICATED 87

CHAPTER 13: DECODING A WOMAN 91

CHAPTER 14: WOMEN AND ANXIETY 99

CHAPTER 15: A MAN'S LEADERSHIP 105

CHAPTER 16: LEARNING TO FOLLOW 109

Part 5: The Wonder of a Man

TRUST AND RESPECT 113

CHAPTER 17: NOT REALLY THAT SIMPLE 117

CHAPTER 18: CREATED WITH PURPOSE 127

CHAPTER 19: STAGES OF A MAN'S LIFE 137

CHAPTER 20: RESPECT THE MAN CAVE 145

CHAPTER 21: WHAT A MAN NEEDS 149

CHAPTER 22: HOME IMPROVEMENT 163

CHAPTER 23: LEARNING TO LEAD 171

Part 6: Life at the Tower of Babel

SPEAKING DIFFERENT LANGUAGES 175

CHAPTER 24: COMMUNICATION STYLES 179

CHAPTER 25: THE ROLE OF EMOTIONS AND
UNDERSTANDING THE STONE WALL 185

CHAPTER 26: SEX MEANS MORE THAN YOU REALIZE 195

Part 7: Submission in the 21st Century

AN OLD-FASHIONED IDEA 201

CHAPTER 27: THE BEAUTY OF THE FEMININE 203

CHAPTER 28: THE PASSION OF THE MASCULINE 207

Conclusion: The Perfect Partnership

BETTER THAN EDEN 213

Bibliography

Acknowledgments

My Beloved Savior: Thank you for Your Promises to me. Because of You, my path is straight, my lot secure.

My Parents: Thank you for my life – and for valuable lessons about its complexity, as well as its brevity.

My Three Sons: You've inspired me to learn about men. But mostly you've made me proud to be your mom.

My Students & Clients: Thanks for letting me participate in your Romantic Journey. What a blessing to get to see the Lord heal you … and grow you to be more like Him!

My Ministry Team: All this couldn't happen without your loyal support. Thanks for being with me through so many Upgrades. Things have been much smoother with your help than they otherwise would have been.

My Dearest Fred: I've always sensed the Lord's Heart in your Love Story. You bring His joy and blessing to life, and I'm so happy that you get me. Dancing with you is Divine Pleasure … because you're the Absolute Best!

I know the plans I have for you. They will stretch you. They are stretching you now. My plans are for your good and the only way you will be truly happy. Trust me. You are more dear and precious to me than you realize. I put those desires in your heart, and I am the only one who can fulfill them. Walk closely to me. You cannot screw this up. You cannot even delay it when you become fearful because I'm at work in your anxious times, too. Do not let shame rule over you. Do not listen to those lies. I will turn your mourning into dancing. You will face challenges, and you will overcome them all. Watch me. Watch what I do next. You're going to love this one!

Love,
Papa

Your love story matters.

It matters because it belongs to you.
It's what you know and where you live.

Mostly, it matters to God.

What happened to you growing up matters because it's
how you learned about Life and Love

... and God.

Your story has taught you a lot about who you are,
and it's taught you about other people.

Some of what you've learned is true.
Some isn't.

That's what this book is about.

Then you will know the truth,
and the truth will set you free."
~ John 8:32

Lord, you alone are my portion and my cup;
you make my lot secure.

The boundary lines have fallen for me in pleasant places;
surely I have a delightful inheritance.

I will praise the Lord, who counsels me;
even at night my heart instructs me.

I keep my eyes always on the Lord.
With him at my right hand, I will not be shaken.

~ Psalm 16:5-8

Chapter 1

ONCE UPON A TIME

She was 14 and alone. The kitchen sink was full of sewage. No one knew, but her ... and the Lord.

Junior high had been a struggle for her, as it is for many a lonely teenager. But her experience in 9th grade had rocked everything in her world. The pain of her shame was so sharp she couldn't sleep. Night after night, she'd stay up 'til the wee hours, crying – sobbing – because she didn't fit in. And she never would.

She'd wanted so badly to fit in. But she was poor. Very poor. Living in a middleclass neighborhood. Pretending she was middleclass. But she wasn't. How many of her friends knew that? Only the few who'd dared to enter her house.

From the outside, the family home seemed quaint – some might even say it was charming. Yellow unpainted stucco that, seen up close, looked like thick cornbread batter, dolloped and swirled in a more-or-less uniform pattern. Perhaps the oldest structure on the block, its uniqueness stood out among the rows of neatly painted white houses that lined both sides of the street in a very quiet neighborhood. French doors led from the small veranda into the living room on one side and into the dining room on the adjacent side, adding to its enchanting ambience.

If you looked closely at sunny reflections in its huge picture window, you'd see wavy places, revealing the fact that it had been installed a long time before its present tenant had been born.

The grass was green enough, except for the scattering of bright dandelions, which always seemed to pop up in defiance within just a few hours of being mowed down. A closer look revealed that the lawn's rich color was the result of a thick combination of clover, broadleaf, and volunteer grasses that had drifted onto the lot from other, more intentional plantings over the years.

The inside, however, told a different story. The whole place reeked of wet wallpaper. Layers and layers of ancient wallpaper that someone had tried unsuccessfully to strip away. Here and there the bare plaster revealed an old and now-ugly past ... stained with yellowed paste, chipped in places, and sometimes revealing the rough surface of the lathe underneath.

No central air. No central furnace. Only a gas stove that stood on the weathered wooden floor in the dining room. The kitchen cabinets, painted with thick ivory enamel, were no longer squarely connected with their doors. Behind the kitchen stove and the hot water heater that stood next to it, someone had attempted to pretty it all by tacking up a large piece of bright yellow linoleum trimmed with broad black stripes that made its crookedness all the more apparent. Nothing matched.

The dark hardwood floors of the living room and bedrooms no longer shined. Their varnish had worn away decades before. The stairs creaked. The lighting was dim. Dark and lonely. Hot in the summer and cold in the winter. No wonder she escaped so often ... sometimes to neighbors'. Sometimes to her only friend's house. Mostly to her church.

She felt safe at church. She knew it's where she belonged.

When she was younger and lived on the other side of town, she'd ridden the Sunday School bus with her older brother. They'd walk two blocks to stand on the corner in front of the Christian Bookstore and pitch pennies while they waited to be picked up. Back then, she only got to go on an occasional Sunday morning.

Thanks to an urban renewal project, however, they had to move to another house, which was back in the old neighborhood. The best thing about it: Now church was just six blocks from home. Before the family owned a car, she'd walk there and back three times each and every week – Sunday morning services, Sunday evening services, and Wednesday night prayer meetings.

The summer she was 12, she left church shortly after dark to walk home. She remembered that it was that particular June because she was wearing the polka dot blouse and matching wraparound skirt she'd make in 7th grade home economics that spring. Ever cautious about her surroundings, she watched and listened as she headed for home.

Just a block or two from the church, she heard footsteps behind her and looked over her shoulder. It was a man in a checkered shirt. Not wanting to appear afraid, she turned her head back in the direction she was going and quickened her steps, but only slightly so as to appear calmer than she actually felt. Kansas was always rainy in June, and the sidewalks had puddles here and there – mostly small, but some large. She lengthened her stride to make it over one of them – at the same instant the man did.

He wrapped his arm around her neck, slapping his hand tightly over her mouth, and commanded, "Don't scream."

Then he yanked her purse from her hand and took off. She didn't know in which direction. Her heart was pounding so hard she couldn't think. As soon as the man had let her go, she began screaming at the top of her lungs. Instinctively, she headed back to the church. Visibly shaken and out of breath, she ran into the foyer where several adults were still visiting. Her Sunday School teacher offered her comfort as she told the story. The police were called, and the pastor gave her a ride home. She didn't sleep well for months. Lots of months.

Now she was 14 … and living alone. The kitchen sink was full of sewage. No one knew, but her … and the Lord. Instead of crying, she plunged. And plunged some more. And as she plunged, she sang aloud every hymn she'd ever learned. *How Great Thou Art. Savior, Like a Shepherd Lead Us. Glorious Freedom.* All four verses of every song she knew.

> Sing the wondrous love of Jesus
> Sing his mercy and his grace
> In the mansions bright and blessed
> He'll prepare for us a place.
>
> When we all get to Heaven
> What a day of rejoicing that will be
> When we all see Jesus
> We'll sing and shout the victory.

Instead of singing and plunging her way through her fears, she should have told someone so they could call a plumber. It all seems pointless now. Or does it? How could she have made it through such a dark time without the Lord?

Many times throughout the years, life struggles would cause her to question the reliability of His love for her. But she always knew He was there.

I know this story well because it's mine.

However, it's only one chapter of my story … a chapter that had its origins in early life experiences and beliefs I'd held about who I was.

Papa, why does the thought of that sink full of sewage still make me cry – after all these years?

That has been your life. You tried to handle it on your own. And you praised me through it all. You were afraid, and the plunging gave you something to do.

The important part – the part I loved about that time – was listening to your praises. Never stop praising me! That is your well-spring of life!

Love,
Papa

How Firm a Foundation

How firm a foundation, ye saints of the Lord,
Is laid for your faith in His excellent word!
What more can He say than to you He hath said –
To you who for refuge to Jesus have fled?

"Fear not, I am with thee, oh, be not dismayed,
For I am thy God, and will still give thee aid;
I'll strengthen thee, help thee, and cause thee to stand,
Upheld by My gracious, omnipotent hand.

"When through the deep waters I call thee to go,
The rivers of sorrow shall not overflow;
For I will be with thee thy trouble to bless,
And sanctify to thee thy deepest distress.

"When through fiery trials thy pathway shall lie,
My grace, all-sufficient, shall be thy supply;
The flame shall not harm thee; I only design
Thy dross to consume and thy gold to refine.

"The soul that on Jesus doth lean for repose,
I will not, I will not, desert to his foes;
That soul, though all hell should endeavor to shake,
I'll never, no never, no never forsake."

~ John Keith, 1787

HOW TO WRITE A LOVE STORY

And now these three remain: faith, hope and love.
But the greatest of these is love.
~ 1 Corinthians 13:13

There's a Love Story inside each of us. Our Heavenly Father put it there Himself. However, the father of lies has been messing with our minds since ... well, for a very long time. He tells us that we're not loveable and/or that other people don't or won't love us. And he gets away with it for awhile, mostly because we don't know or fully realize the Truth.

My Love Story started like this ...

I was born a blue-eyed blonde who was the apple of her daddy's eye. But shortly before I turned 3, my mom packed her friend's car with some essential belongings and left town with my older brother and me ... while my dad was at work. He had no idea what was coming. None of us did.

We were always safe, and Mom took very good care of us. But for most of my life, I experienced a haunting loneliness that I couldn't explain and didn't understand until more than 37 years later. My mother had kept me from my father. She had been abused as a child, and she was very confused about men and their behavior. She adored my three uncles, but didn't really trust any other men ... including my dad.

So she poured herself into being a mom and helping others. A very creative woman, she spent her days cooking and baking and sewing beautiful dresses for me with all kinds of ribbons and bows. How I loved to dress up! But life wasn't always simple, and most lessons were painful.

Being from a divorced family was much more unique in the 1950s than it is now, and apparently something for a child to be ashamed of. I didn't realize that until my Bluebird Troop visited our local radio station when I was 7. The announcer engaged in a live interview with each of the girls. I was so energetic – all twirls and smiles – and so excited to get to be on the radio. When the man came to me, he asked the same questions he had asked of the others, but there seemed to be something very wrong with my answers …

> "What's your name?"
> "Debby"
> "What does your daddy do?"
> "Oh, I don't have a daddy."

The expression on the nice announcer's face changed drastically, and he quickly removed the microphone from in front of me and started talking to the next Bluebird. I was immediately flooded with an overwhelming sense of shame.

It was clear to me that I'd said something terribly wrong, but no one told me what it was. And I was too afraid to ask. So I filed the experience away under an enduring belief about myself: "There's something drastically wrong with you, but no one will tell you what it is. No one will give you the slightest clue. You'll have to figure it out for yourself."

I've never forgotten that day, nor the sadness of my dad's absence. In my little-girl mind, he'd left me for unknowable reasons, setting the stage for my belief about my perceived faults and my conclusion that I would always end up alone.

Everyone Knows the Plot

Although Fairy Tales get a bum rap, there's always a part of the story that resonates with our reality. And that's exactly why so many stories have endured over the centuries.

That's also why so many of us "Hopefuls" love modern-day romantic movies. We adore a "meet cute" at the beginning ... with all the excitement and hope of a new relationship!

Next, the boy wins the girl ... or at least gets her attention. Then he screws up ... or at least she thinks he did. And the rest is about getting her back. Which all happens in less than two hours ... unless we're talking about a made-for-TV miniseries. Or Real Life. Then it takes a little longer.

Which Prince or Princess are you?

As you might imagine, I readily identify with Cinderella. I'd remembered to drop my slipper at the Ball. But I had a hard time believing my Prince would actually come to my house looking for the girl with the foot that fit.

Because of all the lies I'd learned about myself, I found myself willing – on more than one occasion – to settle for whatever frog showed up in front of me.

Of course, there were some potentially good guys in the mix, too. But their lack of maturity tended to make them act more like frogs than princes. Go figure.

The Number One Lie

So there you have it. More than likely, you've had similar identity issues ... also based on your early life experiences. Lies about yourself, to be sure, but also about the opposite sex. These issues can limit our romantic success by clouding our understanding of who we are and why we're here.

As you contemplate your own story – past, present, and future – I pray that you'll see the Father's loving hand in it. No one can change what happened, but you can gain a better understanding by allowing your Heavenly Father to show you the Truth about yourself.

The Beauty of You

In the beginning, God created us and established his own particular order for things. He knew it'd go sideways. No big surprise to Him that we'd have trouble with obedience. That is, we'd want life on our own terms ... until we could fully comprehend the Beauty of a life lived on His terms.

Our Father is motivated by Love. Indeed, He *is* Love. And in His Love, He says ...

> *"For I know the plans I have for you," declares the Lord,*
> *"plans to prosper you and not to harm you,*
> *plans to give you hope and a future.*
> *Then you will call on me and come and pray to me,*
> *and I will listen to you. You will seek me and find me*
> *when you seek me with all your heart. I will be found*
> *... and will bring you back to the place*
> *from which I carried you into exile."*
> *~ Jeremiah 29:11-14*

As we will see in *Part 2, Our Father's Love Story*, He loved Adam and Eve from the start. And when they disobeyed, He already had a Plan to bring about their Redemption. Although He cast them from the Garden He'd created and sent them into exile, His desire was – and always is – to seek and redeem that which is lost.

So let's listen to His Story and use it as our model for how to write our own beautiful Love Story with Him as Co-Author! Each and every day He will use your down-to-earth desires and longings for Romance to help you understand His Great Passion for you as His Beloved. And your new Love Story promises to be filled with Miraculous Adventures ... and a Happy Ending ... guaranteed!

Yes, it will be Romantic! Very Romantic!

First, it's about God's enduring affection for and attention to you as His beloved child. In fact, your life is about learning that you are far more dear and precious to Him than you will ever realize ... even on your Best Day. And that He has a magnificent plan for your life from this day forward.

In fact, His Plan for Love was already in place before the foundations of the earth (1 Peter 1:20). That's a really, really long time. And He's really, really, really dedicated to letting you know just exactly how much He loves you!

Second, He has chosen Romance in Marriage as the earthly example of His Love ... His best illustration of how much Jesus loves and cares for us.

> *Husbands, love your wives, just as Christ loved*
> *the church and gave himself up for her to make her holy,*
> *cleansing her by the washing with water through the word,*
> *and to present her to himself as a radiant church,*
> *without stain or wrinkle or any other blemish,*
> *but holy and blameless.*
> ~ Ephesians 5:25-27

With that in mind, I'm guessing our ability to get things right in Marriage must be pretty important to Him. That'll mean He's highly invested to be in the process with us. That's Good News!

Therefore, this book is filled with lots and lots of practical information – based on Scripture and findings of scientific research – richly seasoned with God's extravagant love, joy, peace, patience, kindness, goodness, faithfulness, gentleness, and self-control (Galatians 5:22-23).

My purpose is to help you identify the Truth about yourself and others ... and to give you instant encouragement in the process of life ... which is mostly about love. Actually, life is *only* about love. In fact, it's all that matters.

Love Divine, All Loves Excelling

Love divine, all loves excelling,
Joy of Heav'n to earth come down;
Fix in us thy humble dwelling;
All thy faithful mercies crown!
Jesus, Thou art all compassion,
Pure unbounded love Thou art;
Visit us with Thy salvation,
Enter every trembling heart.

Breathe, O breathe Thy loving Spirit
Into every troubled breast!
Let us all in Thee inherit;
Let us find that second rest.
Take away our bent to sinning;
Alpha and Omega be;
End of faith, as its beginning,
Set our hearts at liberty.

Finish, then, Thy new creation;
Pure and spotless let us be;
Let us see Thy great salvation
Perfectly restored in Thee;
Changed from glory into glory,
Till in Heav'n we take our place,
Till we cast our crowns before Thee,
Lost in wonder, love, and praise.

~ Charles Wesley, 1747

Part 2
Our Father's Love Story

THE GARDEN OF EDEN

Love

Who's not a hopeless romantic
deep down in their secret soul?
Even the most jaded
falls under its beguiling control.

A star filled night and a golden moon
hypnotize and tease
casting lovers under the spell
of kisses from a summer breeze.

The promise of the unknown
beckons even the most shy
do you dare step forward in faith
or let love's whisper pass you by.

For a simple dance all by yourself
can certainly be done
but the dance of love is far more complex
because two must dance as one.

~ Marilyn Sweet, 2012

God must be a baseball fan.

Right after I gave birth to my third son, the doctor suggested that I must be going for a basketball team. My immediate thought was, "I'd rather have a baseball team. Not because I want nine sons. But because I like baseball better."

Some thoughts are better left unexpressed.

Anyway ... God must be a baseball fan, too. Because He decided to start the Bible in The Big Inning.

Most couples think of Romance in the beginning, which to many of us is "The Big Inning." That is, we think more about the beauty and excitement of the Wedding, not realizing how much we need to learn to insure the beauty and excitement of our Romance will last for a life time.

Unfortunately, our culture – and even much of our spiritual training – has taught us to believe that we are not intended to enjoy a Lifelong Romance. Love, yes. Romance, no.

Some highly educated folks – who you would think might know better – have told us outright that God isn't interested our happiness. He only cares about our holiness. And that your mate is in your life – not to bring you unbounded joy and pleasure – but to test you.

Huh? So God put your mate in your life to *irritate* you into submission? If that's true, better to remain single, eh?

And Romance is just a lot of nonsense – a fantasy designed to distract us from the reality of who we're supposed to be?

No Romance??? Seriously.

Most of us have been taught that Romance naturally fades and gives way to .... What? Boredom? Who wants that??? But that's what most couples settle for ... that is, if they are really committed to *sticking it out* together. What a bummer!

Romance is meant to grow and blossom – to become deeper and more satisfying over a life time. Both Scripture and the findings of scientific research tell us that we all strive to love and to be loved, which is the greatest of gifts.

Plus, Our God is the Original Romantic! Or have you all forgotten the Great Romances of the Bible. Adam and Eve? Abraham and Sarah? Isaac and Rebekah? Jacob and Rachel? Boaz and Ruth? Joseph and Mary?

Yes, I know. Things went wrong in those relationships, too. The ingredients were there, but we know that First Couple blew it for us all. Eve gets most of the blame, of course. And it's all downhill from there. Or is it? Is it possible that those two just set the stage for something Better Than Eden? What an interesting proposition that is!

What if we could learn something very important – and extremely relevant to us – from Adam and Eve's experience? Was there one particular reason the serpent talked to Eve instead of to her husband? And what was Adam thinking? How did his thoughts, feelings, and behavior contribute to the serpent's plan to destroy God's creation?

We are different because God intends us to be.

No, men are not from Mars, and women are not from Venus. Men don't have waffle brains, and women's brains are not made of spaghetti. We are created by – and in the image of – an All-Wise God who made man and woman differently (one from dust, and the other from a rib). And He intends for us to remain different.

To understand our differences, we'll review The Big Inning, what goes wrong, and our consequences. Then we're going to explore what happens when Heaven Comes to Earth! It's just as amazing as is all that the Lord has planned for your Marriage ... whether you even have one yet or not!

> *Nothing is impossible with God.*
> ~ Genesis 18:14a

Chapter 3

IN THE BEGINNING

So God created mankind in his own image,
in the image of God he created them;
male and female he created them.
~ Genesis 1:27

As a young wife, I remember longing to have children of my own. And for some reason that only God knows, I just wanted sons. So that's what He gave me. Three times.

I don't recall ever asking the Lord to give me teenagers. But at some point, that's what I ended up with.

I wonder if that's how God felt about Adam and Eve, too. He could have created whatever He wanted. And He did.

At the peak of His creativity, the Lord wanted to make another Someone – a Someone who would bear His likeness. And the Someone He made would have a natural need and desire for Him – and a need for a Someone of his own.

And like teenagers, they would rebel. But He had already devised a Great Plan to get them out of the trouble He knew they would get themselves into. It's apparent from the beginning that we're better at getting ourselves into stuff than we are at getting ourselves out of it.

You know the story, right?

God creates the Heavens and the Earth – from Nothing. You and I can't imagine Nothing. For us, there has always been Something. Scientists claim they've figured out how to make Something out of Nothing. However, they need a lot of special equipment to get it done.

God doesn't need any special equipment. He just says, "Let there be." And there is!

For instance, He says, "Let there be light." And suddenly there is ... both light and darkness. That is, Day and Night. Day One. He's pleased with His work.

On Day Two, His "Let there be" separates Sky from Water. So far, so good. That's how He sees it.

On Day Three, He really gets busy with Land and Seas, and Plants and Trees. All come into being at the sound of His voice. And He sees again that it's all good.

Day Four brings Sun, Moon, and Stars. So far, still good. He's setting the stage for Romance now, don't you think?

Day Five comes with Sea Creatures and Winged Birds. All good, of course. But this time, the Lord gives a blessing and instructions to what He has created.

> *God blessed them and said,*
> *"Be fruitful and increase in number and fill the water in the seas,*
> *and let the birds increase on the earth."*
> ~ Genesis 1:22

On Day Six He creates Land Animals. Of course, He saves His Best for last. He creates Man and Woman in His Image – to rule over the Fish and the Birds, the Animals and the Creepy Crawlers. And He gives them Plenty to eat.

God blessed them and said to them,
"Be fruitful and increase in number; fill the earth and subdue it.
Rule over the fish in the sea and the birds in the sky and
over every living creature that moves on the ground."
~ Genesis 1:28

Are you beginning to see a pattern here? The Lord blesses us, commands fruitfulness, and expects us to increase. Plus, He gives man dominion over Creation. *All* of Creation!

This is where the Story gets really good. I love the way the Lord shows us more detail about just how He creates Adam. He tells us man is formed from the dust of the ground, and that God Himself breathes into Adam the Breath of Life.

Then He sets the man down – smack in the middle of Eden – with enjoyable and fruitful work to do (pun intended). Adam is now the Resident Gardener with amazing freedom. He can eat anything he wants ... except for the fruit of the Tree of Knowledge of Good and Evil. That sounds easy enough, yes? I'm sure Adam thought so, too.

Now we get to the really good part. Well, it's actually the no-so-good part. That is, what is not-so-good at that point – compared to everything else, which is good – is that Adam is alone. He needs his own Someone. So God does surgery ... while Adam's sleeping, of course. The Lord removes a rib to create his Someone – Someone just for him.

Can you imagine Adam's excitement when he wakes up? A totally cool setup – just for him. He already has the whole world at his fingertips. Lots of food. Freedom to putter around in a lavish Garden. Then God gives him a wife, too? She's the perfect addition to make his life the Paradise God wanted him to enjoy.

That'd be better than having control of the remote, don't you think? Besides, they were the only two people on Earth at that point ... and the football hadn't been invented yet.

Just think about it. Adam has everything going for him. The Garden is pure pleasure for all his senses. Sight, sound, fragrance, taste, touch. Nevertheless, the Lord thinks of one thing more He wants for Adam.

God sees Adam's need, and gives him the Perfect Partner. His Bride is there to rescue him from being alone. Now he has a companion – Someone like him – only different – very different. Someone with whom he can enjoy the pleasures of God's Creation. Plus they are both totally naked. She's beautiful beyond words ... and totally irresistible.

Adam names her Eve.

He can hardly believe his luck! No competition anywhere. Complete Freedom, and no 2-hour commute to work 5 days a week. Plus Endless Rapture with his Sweet Companion. Sex with her whenever he's in the mood – which I'm guessing is pretty much all the time.

And Eve's only desire is to be beside her Dearest Husband, to give herself completely to him, and to bask in his love. She experiences his desire for her as pure Joy and Bliss.

No meals to cook. No dishes to wash. No house to clean. No kids to pick up after. And no dirty laundry to do. Only a totally Hot Husband who adores her. Lucky girl!

Bonus! God Himself comes down from Heaven in the cool of the evening and walks with them in the Garden. And none of them even care if He walks in on their Lovemaking. After all, it was His idea in the first place, right?

The Creation Story is about the Lord's goodness and how He romances both Adam and Eve with His Loving Presence (Romans 2:4). But soon, something goes terribly wrong ...

Chapter 4

FALLING FOR THE LIE

Now the serpent was more crafty than any
of the wild animals the Lord God had made.
~ Genesis 3:1a

So here's where we are so far in the Story. God has created the Heavens and the Earth. Day and Night. Sky and Water. Land and Seas, and Plants and Trees. Sun, Moon, and Stars. Sea Creatures, Winged Birds, and Land Animals.

The Lord takes extra special care in His creation of Adam. Then He creates Eve and gives her to him. He is her Dearest Husband, and she is his Sweet Companion. The two of them are enjoying one another immensely in the Garden, and God comes down to pay them a visit once each day.

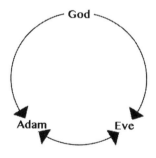

Whatever they need, it's already provided by the Lord.

We can't imagine – even in our wildest dreams – just how perfect the world is for them in the Garden. But we can try. Because the traces of a deep level of desire and satisfaction linger in our hearts and in our souls. Indeed, we long for it. We long for that kind of connection with our mates and with our Creator. Yes, that desire still lies deep within us somewhere. We are created in His image, remember?

Alas, Life is beautiful for the First Couple. All their needs are met in the Garden. They're fully enjoying one another, and taking daily walks with their Creator. He only requires One Thing ...

> *And the Lord God commanded the man,*
> *"You are free to eat from any tree in the garden;*
> *but you must not eat from the tree*
> *of the knowledge of good and evil,*
> *for when you eat from it you will certainly die."*
> ~ Genesis 2:16-17

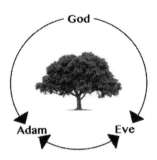

That seemed like a totally reasonable request to Adam, so he gave it no further thought, other than to relay the message to Eve. He had no concerns about anything. He had more than enough food. Enjoyable work to do. A beautiful place to hang out, and a Sweet Companion with whom to share it.

What more did he need than that?

Eve hears the message and accepts it as Truth. No reason to doubt anything. She's having a great time, too, remember?

All they know is the Lord's goodness. They have no doubts and are enjoying a Fearless Life. They are living in complete freedom and have many choices about what they want to do and how they want to enjoy each day. Everything is perfect.

Meanwhile, in a remote part of the Garden ...

The enemy is plotting to spoil God's Creation. The Lord, of course, knows he's there because even the enemy is a created being.

An angel so impressed with himself – his own beauty, intelligence, power, and position – that he wanted all the glory and honor to go with it. That is, he had enough self-pride to believe he deserved to be God. Cast from Heaven due to his arrogance, he lost his identity as a Morning Star, and became the Adversary – the enemy who seeks his revenge by distorting God's created order.

Adam and Eve, however, are unaware of his presence.

So one day, the two of them are strolling through Paradise when they encounter the crafty serpent, who strikes up a conversation with Eve. The enemy knows that the primacy of her emotions will make her an easier target than Adam.

> *He said to the woman, "Did God really say,*
> *'You must not eat from any tree in the garden'?"*
> ~ Genesis 3:1b

As it turns out, he is right about her. Eve is an easy mark. She replies that God said they can eat the fruit of any tree except the one in the middle of the Garden. She goes further and says that if they even *touch* the tree, they will die, which God did not say. The serpent clearly has her attention.

"You will not certainly die," the serpent said to the woman. "For God knows that when you eat from it your eyes will be opened, and you will be like God, knowing good and evil."
~ Genesis 3:4-5

Eve's emotions kick into overdrive. She gets more than a little anxious about the perceived quality of the life she's living. She begins to doubt the goodness of God and his provision. And rather than following her husband as her authority, she gives her attention to the serpent instead.

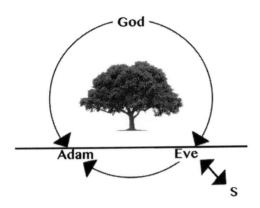

The evidence is right there in front of her, and she reasons. "The fruit of the tree does look good. Really good. Could it be God is holding out on us? What if that stuff the Lord told Adam about that delicious-looking fruit isn't actually true? Is God denying us good things? Is He refusing to make us fully aware of all that we might become? Is He refusing us all we could enjoy … all that we deserve? Life seems great. That's true. But what if we could have more? What if we could be more? What if we could be like God?"

She evidently forgets that they are already like God. Or did she miss that part of The Big Inning?

So God created mankind in his own image, in the image of God he created them; *male and female he created them.*
~ Genesis 1:27

"Yes, the serpent must be right," she reasons. She can see it with her own eyes. So she ignores Adam – doesn't even ask for his input – and takes matters into her own hands. She falls for The Lie, takes a bite of the fruit, then gives it to her husband who is there with her.

Ignoring God's authority, Adam chooses to please his wife, listens to Eve's reasoning, yields his authority as husband, and decides to follow his wife's lead instead.

He reaches out and takes the fruit into his own hand.

And without so much as a moment's hesitation ... without questioning his wife's leadership ... without claiming his dominion over the serpent ... or most importantly, checking in with his Creator ... Adam takes a bite, too.

Then all hell breaks loose ... so to speak.

Suddenly Adam and Eve realize they are naked. They're hit hard – broadsided – by painful emotions they were never meant to experience. Their shame is immediate and intense.

They both feel an overwhelming and unfamiliar need ... the need to cover themselves. So they quickly sew some leaves together to make clothes.

And they hide from their Creator.

Trust and Obey

When we walk with the Lord in the light of His Word,
What a glory He sheds on our way!
While we do His good will, He abides with us still,
And with all who will trust and obey.

Trust and obey, for there's no other way
To be happy in Jesus, but to trust and obey.

Not a shadow can rise, not a cloud in the skies,
But His smile quickly drives it away;
Not a doubt or a fear, not a sigh or a tear,
Can abide while we trust and obey.

Not a burden we bear, not a sorrow we share,
But our toil He doth richly repay;
Not a grief or a loss, not a frown or a cross,
But is blessed if we trust and obey.

But we never can prove the delights of His love
Until all on the altar we lay;
For the favor He shows, for the joy He bestows,
Are for them who will trust and obey.

Then in fellowship sweet we will sit at His feet,
Or we'll walk by His side in the way;
What He says we will do, where He sends we will go;
Never fear, only trust and obey.

~ John H. Sammis, 1887

Chapter 5

LIVING UNDER THE CURSE

But the Lord God called to the man,
"Where are you?"
~ Genesis 3:9

Brace yourselves. This part's going to sound really familiar.

God comes looking for Adam. What makes that man think it's possible to hide from God? The Lord already knows what's taken place, of course.

Adam blames Eve. "That woman you gave me ...."

Eve blames the serpent. "The serpent deceived me."

So the serpent gets the honor of receiving the first curse. The Lord says he'll crawl around on his belly and eat dirt for the remainder of his life. There will be ongoing hostility between the serpent and the woman, as well as between his offspring and hers.

Then his ultimate doom is foretold. The woman's offspring will crush the serpent's head, and the serpent will strike her offspring's heel.

And there is Jesus. We already know how Our Father's Love Story will end! He knew we would get ourselves into

Big Trouble. And He knew we wouldn't be able to get ourselves out of it.

But Eve doesn't get out of this divine encounter without her own set of consequences. The Lord informs her that she'll experience severe pain in giving birth to her children. That's bad enough, but that's not the most difficult part!

The Lord also tells her that her desire will always be for her husband, and that she will try – without success – to retain the leadership role she took from him in the Garden. However – from here on out – her husband will resist all her efforts to control, manage, and fix him.

And there it is! The invention of the football isn't far off!

Adam gets his own set of consequences. Because he chose to listen to his wife instead of to the Lord's commandment, he no longer gets a free ride when it comes to providing food for himself and his family. His work was pleasant before his disobedience. His work had always been fruitful. But now, he's going to have to work really, really hard – without much to show for it.

So there you have it … the 2-hour commute to work 5 days a week. The earth will no longer readily produce food, but will become his ongoing struggle with thorns and thistles. And when he dies, he's going to be buried in it.

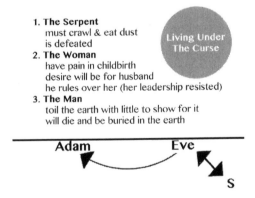

1. **The Serpent**
   must crawl & eat dust
   is defeated

Living Under The Curse

2. **The Woman**
   have pain in childbirth
   desire will be for husband
   he rules over her (her leadership resisted)

3. **The Man**
   toil the earth with little to show for it
   will die and be buried in the earth

Adam   Eve

S

I told you it would sound familiar, didn't I?

My experience as a couples psychologist has me convinced that this is exactly where most couples are living today. Most of us keep acting as though we are still sinners living under the curse. We don't live like we're the saints we're called to be as God's redeemed sons and daughters.

Our true identity is in Christ.

We need to have an understanding that our true identity is in Christ. An old pastor once said: "I have always found it interesting that before we are saved, the enemy tries to convince us that we're *not* guilty of any wrongdoing. Then once we are saved, he spends all of his energy convincing us that we *are* guilty."

Go figure. But if it works, I guess you don't have any need to change your tactics. At this point in history, the enemy seems to have succeeded in convincing us that there's no hope for having happy, healthy relationships – especially when it comes to Romance and Marriage.

First, we need to stop playing the Blame Game.

That's one of the enemy's favorite pastimes. All he does is whisper one of his lies in your ear – and you begin to see your mate as The Problem.

Then he just sits back and relaxes – because now you're both out of commission in the Kingdom. And he's got his eye on your kids next ...

Meanwhile back in the Garden ...

Even in announcing the Curse, God provides and protects His beloved couple. Knowing that their leaf garments will not be sufficient, He sacrifices an animal to provide a more suitable cover for their sin. Another sign of what's ahead in

Our Father's Plan for Love – that is, Jesus' atoning sacrifice that will cover our sin once and for all.

Finally, the Lord casts them from the Garden because He knows that if they are allowed to eat from the Tree of Life, they will live forever in their sinful state.

And He has a much, much better Plan for Adam and Eve – and for all of us – than ending it there!

Read on …

Chapter 6

HEAVEN COMES TO EARTH

For God so loved the world that he gave his one and only Son,
that whoever believes in him shall not perish but have eternal life.
~ John 3:16

Despite what we know from Scripture and have seen in the movies about Jesus' life, death, and resurrection, it's difficult to fully know what life was like for Him. But I imagine He was a normal, happy child who grew into a confident adult. I doubt He ever rebelled against Joseph and Mary.

Can you imagine living next door to their family? You can almost hear the back-and-forth rasp of handsaws cutting fragrant wood and the pounding of His hammer as He creates another Masterpiece with His calloused hands. The laughter of children playing nearby. The sweet aroma of baking bread. His mother's voice calling Him in for dinner.

Yet no one notices anything particularly amazing in Him. Of course, there was that old rumor about His conception. His parents weren't married then, only engaged. But like any gossip, it had probably died down long before He'd become a man. An ordinary man.

Then one day, He's at a Wedding. And the host of the feast runs out of wine … long before the party is over. His mom, who knows the Truth about Him, sets Him up. It seems

He's not especially happy about that, but He steps in and saves the day nonetheless.

Miracle #1: Water turns into wine. Not just any wine. It's like the best wine ever. Instantly. No planting the vineyard. No waiting for it to bear fruit. No working the winepress. No aging in wooden barrels. No wineskins. No waiting. No drama. Simply the best wine ever. Instantly.

Nothing is impossible with God. Remember that.

Jesus then meets up with John and gets Himself baptized. The Father loves it and announces to everyone how pleased He is with His Son.

Then Jesus heads out into the desert for 40 days of fasting. And guess-who shows up. That old fallen angel – the one known as the adversary – evidently has no idea Who he is trying to mess with out there. So he pulls a few tricks out of his infamous bag of lies. Jesus doesn't fall for any of them. Instead, He quotes Scripture.

And the enemy takes off. He can't stand against the Truth. Never has. Never will. Remember that.

Jesus begins His ministry. He goes "around doing good and healing all who [are] under the power of the devil because God [is] with him" (Acts 10:38b).

Soon He's very popular. Which doesn't sit at all well with the religious leaders. It's time for the Passover, and they're getting really worried about Trouble in River City. Not that Jesus is opening a pool hall, of course. He's just messing with their teachings.

He says dangerous stuff like, "You have heard that it was said .... But I tell you that ...." (Matthew 5:27-28).

Despite what the people are saying – or maybe because of what the people are saying – the religious leaders don't like Him at all. And they try to trap Him – more than once.

Can you imagine? Trying to catch the Son of God doing something wrong? How crazy is that? Of course, they don't have a clue that He is Who He is. They think He's just some troublemaker dude from Nazareth. Boy, are they wrong!

At the peak of His popularity, Jesus rides into Jerusalem on a donkey. His disciples are more than pumped about His Kingdom. The people spread their coats on the road ahead of Him. Some are waving palm branches ...

> *The crowds that went ahead of him and those that followed*
> *shouted, "Hosanna to the Son of David!"*
> *"Blessed is he who comes in the name of the Lord!"*
> *"Hosanna in the highest heaven!"*
> ~ Matthew 21:9

Well, you can just imagine how well that goes over with the religious leaders. Their plot thickens.

Jesus has supper with His disciples and shares disturbing news. One who's eating with them will betray Him. Jesus will die, and they're all going to scatter. They can hardly believe their ears. But it's true.

He prays while they wait. He's betrayed and arrested there in the Garden. An interesting place for that to happen, yes?

His trial is mockery, and He is beaten severely. That same crowd – the one that hailed Him into Jerusalem just a few days before – chooses a criminal to be released for Passover. When asked what to do with Jesus, the people shout,

> *Crucify Him! ... Crucify Him!*
> ~ Matthew 27:22-23

It looks like the enemy is winning. The Son of God's beaten. Literally. But nothing could be farther from the Truth.

Because nothing is impossible with God.

> *"The reason my Father loves me is that I lay down my life – only to take it up again. No one takes it from me, but I lay it down of my own accord. I have authority to lay it down and authority to take it up again. This command I received from my Father."*
> John 10:17-18

So Jesus is crucified, dies, and is buried. But, of course, there's more to Our Father's Love Story than meets the eye. His Plan is working. By paying for our sins, Jesus is buying us back! He declares, *"It is finished"* (John 19:30).

Done. We are redeemed! Free from the bondage of sin and death. And more ...

Easter is the best holiday on the calendar. My favorite part is the congregation's response to the pastor's opening words on Resurrection Sunday:

> Hallelujah! He is Risen!
> He is Risen indeed!

I've been known to go to more than one church on Easter Sunday – as many as three morning services – just so I can hear the Glorious News over and over and over again.

The most moving Easter Service of my life took place when my oldest son was a young adult. We were asked to be part of our church's Easter program: a series of scenes that take place at the foot of the empty cross. We played mother and son – which was a bit of a stretch for us – not because of our relationship, of course. But because neither of us had ever acted in a play. That is, unless you count elementary school programs, which I don't think you can.

We're sitting in the back of the church, incredibly nervous, waiting for the other scenes to play out. My son looks at me and says, "I don't want to do this."

"I don't either," I replied. "Let's go."

But neither of us moved.

We're on. The only two actors in the final scene. The lights come up on my son, looking up at the empty cross in awe.

I enter from stage right, walk up behind him, and say, "I've been looking for you, and I thought you'd be here. It's time to come home, Son."

He tells me about the amazing things that have happened. He joyfully declares, "Jesus has risen from the dead! He's alive, Mother! He's alive!"

After a few minutes of dialogue, my son runs off to share the Good News with anyone who will listen, leaving me standing there alone. I take a few steps forward and look up at the cross, lost in silent wonder. Then the lights dim.

It's very powerful.

That year our church had an empty tomb – a prop we'd used in another production. And on Sunday morning, they set it up the in the parking lot in front of the church. As everyone leaves the service, our director – dressed in her biblical costume – excitedly urges our whole congregation, "Come and see! He's not here! He is Risen!"

I walk over, look into the empty tomb, and immediately tears of joy and wonder flood over my entire being.

And that's the Truth about why I love Easter.

Hallelujah! He is Risen!
He is Risen indeed!

Christ the Lord is Risen Today

Christ the Lord is ris'n today, Alleluia!
Sons of men and angels say, Alleluia!
Raise your joys and triumphs high, Alleluia!
Sing, ye heav'ns, and earth, reply, Alleluia!

Lives again our glorious King, Alleluia!
Where, O death, is now thy sting? Alleluia!
Once He died our souls to save, Alleluia!
Where thy victory, O grave? Alleluia!

Love's redeeming work is done, Alleluia!
Fought the fight, the battle won, Alleluia!
Death in vain forbids His rise, Alleluia!
Christ hath opened paradise, Alleluia!

Soar we now where Christ hath led, Alleluia!
Foll'wing our exalted Head, Alleluia!
Made like Him, like Him we rise, Alleluia!
Ours the cross, the grave, the skies, Alleluia!

~ Charles Wesley, 1739

CHAPTER 7

THE SPIRIT OF TRUTH ABIDES

*Follow God's example, therefore, as dearly loved children
and walk in the way of love, just as Christ loved us and gave
himself up for us as a fragrant offering and sacrifice to God.*
~ Ephesians 5:1-2

Through His finished work on the cross, Jesus brought us back into right relationship with Our Father. Not only that, but when He ascended into Heaven, He promised to never leave us or forsake us (Matthew 28:20). And He promised to send us the Holy Spirit to be Our Comforter and Our Guide.

In the beginning, God came down and walked in the Garden with Adam and Eve (Genesis 3:8). And there are many times in Scripture where the Lord says He'll always be with His people (Deuteronomy 31:6).

However, in the gift of the Holy Spirit, we see the first time He establishes His residence *within* us.

*And I will ask the Father, and he will give you
another advocate to help you and be with you forever –
the Spirit of truth. The world cannot accept him,
because it neither sees him nor knows him.
But you know him, for he lives with you and will be in you.*
~ John 14:16-17

The Holy Spirit provides us with the wisdom and revelation (Ephesians 1:17) we need to reestablish the created order Our Father planned for us. We are redeemed – as well as in the process of being redeemed. We cannot hope to bring back the created order merely through the wisdom of mental health professionals who are available to help us *figure things out*, but because we have the Holy Spirit within us so we can *find things out* (Matthew 7:7)!

With Scripture to tell us what that created order looks like, and the Holy Spirit at work within us, our relationships can become *even better* than they were with Adam and Eve. And it was pretty great back then ... before the Fall, that is.

I love Paul's letter to the Ephesians.

Maybe because it was the topic of my first women's Bible study. At any rate, I still love it as much as I did back in the 1970s. It's all good. But without a doubt, the fifth chapter is my favorite.

At the start of the chapter, the Apostle reminds us we are living our life redeemed. That is, we're now God's children because of what Jesus did on the cross. So we must always remember who we are in Christ and refrain from stuff that isn't good for us. Makes sense to me.

Then he lays out the ground rules for us to get relationships back in order, as they were intended to be when Adam and Eve were living in the Garden. Only better.

Instructions to Christian Households

Using some of the most romantic words in the Bible, Paul describes what the male-female relationship should look and feel like for a pair who have chosen to follow Christ's example as Head, with the Church as His Bride.

> *Submit to one another out of reverence for Christ.*
> ~ Ephesians 5:21

In short, these simple truths teach us how we should engage with one another to be successful in Life ... and in Marriage.

First, Paul instructs us to submit to one another as members of the body of believers in fellowship with one another, which naturally will apply to husbands and wives as well. However, just *how* husbands and wives are to submit to one another is easily – and very frequently – misunderstood in our current culture. And men and women need to work together to get it right before they're even dating!

Basically, Paul tells us that men and women are equal, yet different. Both are created in the Image of God to work together in harmony, and each is designed for a unique role in the relationship. One is creatively designed to lead, and his partner's *trust* and *respect* are essential for him to be able to lead well. The other is creatively designed to follow, and her partner's *love* and *understanding* are essential if she is to follow well.

That's my personal mission – helping couples and singles learn the Truth about what loving Submission looks like in the 21st Century. It doesn't involve acting out extremes on either side, but is a balance of working together as God intends – of learning to dance well.

Dancing is a great metaphor here because it requires that we understand the Truth about one another from God's point of view. We also need to understand the Truth about our own needs and limitations – and the Truth about our partner's needs and limitations.

No doubt, every Christian woman loves the idea of being swept off her feet by a godly man who knows how to lead – gently and confidently, protecting her and guiding her through life. Every Christian woman wants a husband who is willing to die for her, as Christ died for the Church, yes? A woman has no problem submitting to a man she truly believes has her best interest at the forefront of everything he does.

However, many women – even those who are already married to a Christian man – feel like they can only long for this experience, having no idea how they can help translate this dream into their reality.

And a Christian man loves the thought of having a godly woman to lead – a woman who is confident and provides him with gentle feedback about how well he's doing … especially if she's adept at making him look good in the process. What Christian man would not want a wife whose desire is only to please him and be his partner?

The fact is, most men are inwardly unsure of themselves and rarely get the positive feedback they crave – though they rarely, if ever, ask for it.

Learn the Truth About Your Partner

First of all, creating and sustaining a Romance that's healthy will mean you must learn your partner really well.

> Gals, what does he need? What pleases him?
> Guys, what does she want? What makes her smile?

Learning the Truth about another person takes lots of time. Therefore, I've always advised men and women to marry only that person that they're willing to spend the rest of their lives getting to know … because that's how long it will take … an endless and a welcome task … made equally complicated and highly pleasurable due to our differences.

Oh, Joyous Rapture!

In the following sections of this book, I'll show you just exactly *how* and *why* Paul's instructions work … in favor of **both** sexes who want to live out a Blessed Romance. All of this information is based upon the findings of psychological research regarding the psychology of men and relationships.

And if you're a Hopeful Romantic, you're going love it!

Part 3
The Psychology of Relationships

THE STUDY OF ROMANCE

Just as King Solomon did in Old Testament times, we all can learn a lot through our life experiences and observations.

What's True About Us vs. the Truth About Us

Anyone can gather facts about what exists. But just because something is true, doesn't mean it's the Truth. That is, our experiences and observations help us *describe* life. However, simple observation, in and of itself, does not – and indeed cannot – lead us to any conclusions about how things *should* be. For that, we need an accurate understanding of the Truth about who we are – and *Whose* we are – as well as an accurate understanding of God's created order. Otherwise, we risk making really big mistakes by misinterpreting the *meaning* of our experiences and observations.

Observations by Others Can Prove Helpful

A number of researchers (see Bibliography at the end of this book for a detailed list) have studied the process of human development from a psychological perspective, and those who have contributed to the Theory of Attachment have provided us with some easily understood information about who we are, particularly in relationship to one another – and even to our Creator.

The Theory of Attachment was originally used in the study of children and their caregivers. Subsequent researchers began to explore how this theory might also be applied to adult relationships. I prefer to use one of the earlier models of adult attachment because it's easy to understand and will be helpful for our present discussion.

Much to our advantage, psychologists have also conducted more than three decades of research about marriages, so we're going to take a look at their findings as well.

Praise Him! Praise Him!

Praise Him! Praise Him! Jesus, our blessed Redeemer!
Sing, O Earth, His wonderful love proclaim!
Hail Him! Hail Him! Highest archangels in glory;
Strength and honor give to His holy Name!
Like a shepherd, Jesus will guard His children,
In His arms He carries them all day long.

Praise Him! Praise Him! Tell of His excellent greatness;
Praise Him! Praise Him! Ever in joyful song!

Praise Him! Praise Him! Jesus, our blessed Redeemer!
For our sins He suffered, and bled, and died.
He our Rock, our hope of eternal salvation,
Hail Him! Hail Him! Jesus the Crucified.
Sound His praises! Jesus who bore our sorrows,
Love unbounded, wonderful, deep, and strong.

Praise Him! Praise Him! Jesus, our blessed Redeemer!
Heav'nly portals loud with hosannas ring!
Jesus, Savior, reigneth forever and ever;
Crown Him! Crown Him! Prophet and Priest and King!
Christ is coming! Over the world victorious,
Pow'r and glory unto the Lord belong.

~ Fanny Crosby, 1869

Chapter 8

YOUR LONGING FOR LOVE

Taste and see that the Lord is good;
blessed is the one who takes refuge in him.
~ Psalm 34:8

Have you ever been in love? The fact of the matter is, we all fell in love for the first time when we were just tiny babies. If you doubt that, just observe the way an infant looks into his mother's eyes.

How interesting that a newborn's vision is its very best at a distance of seven to ten inches. Which just so happens to be the same distance it is from his eyes to his mom's eyes while she's nursing him.

Is Our Creator Amazing or What?

The Truth is, most of us have had an intimate relationship with someone at least once in our life time. Yes, for most of us, it was Mom.

You may be one whose experience of love was short circuited for one reason or another. But most of us have had at least a taste of love, no matter how brief.

Psychologists say we continue to search for that same depth of emotional connection throughout our lives.

Is love really that hard to find?

Sadly, it can be. Especially when we're unaware of what it takes to create and maintain an intimate connection with someone of the opposite sex. Nevertheless, we're intimately familiar with that longing.

The subject of love – especially the romantic kind – has been the core of art and literature throughout the ages. Even pop songs are primarily about falling in love – usually magically and effortlessly. Or about being "done wrong" or "looking for love" – often in all the wrong places.

So where did this whole concept of Romantic love originate? With our Creator, of course. Did you seriously think I was going to say it was Hallmark's idea?

The Lord had Romance on His mind while He was doing surgery on Adam. It's true that Adam lost something in the process. However, the Lord knew that what he would gain in the process would be Priceless – especially in terms of his lifelong health and happiness.

Whatever in the world made Christians start spreading the rumor that the Lord is no longer interested in our Romance? Or that He doesn't care about our happiness?

Who made up *those* lies? I wonder. Hmmm ...

As noted in Chapter 2, some believe God is disinterested in such adolescent fantasies. Unfortunately, most counselors and pastors seem to believe that as well. They're writing books about how married love isn't intended to be Romantic. That all fades ... evidently. They propose that Romance is just something Hollywood invented.

Really? I thought Romance was a lot older than that!

When I was teaching at Azusa Pacific University, one of my colleagues wanted to refer a student to me for assistance with her research project. Because he knew I was into the Psychology of Men and Romance, he asked if I'd be willing to talk with her. She proposed that movies – especially the romantic ones – perpetuate a dangerous myth that sets people up with unrealistic expectations about love that will always result in painful disappointment.

I told him I'd love to talk with her; however, I disagreed with her assumption. Those romantic movies are successful because they connect to our innate desire for Romantic love – deep, caring, sensual love. In fact, it's a God-given desire.

And those of you who dislike "chick flicks" (which may include a lot of men) probably have other issues, to which I'll allude later on in this book. However, you'll have to put two and two together for yourself for now, as that is a great topic for my next book, which already has a working title. (But don't tell anyone, okay? It'll be our little secret.)

So what evidence do we have that the Lord is still interested in our happiness and Romance? Well, He put those two people together in the Garden – because it wasn't good for Adam to be alone. No, Adam didn't need a housekeeper or someone to wash his clothes and cook his meals. So it must have been something else, yes?

And if you'd like a whole book full of evidence that the Lord is Romantic, check out the Song of Solomon.

Finally, I propose we all have that same longing inside us, no matter how deeply or long ago we may have buried it.

Hope deferred makes the heart sick;
but a longing fulfilled is a well-spring of life.
~ Proverbs 13:12

Come Thou Fount of Every Blessing

Come, Thou Fount of every blessing,
Tune my heart to sing Thy grace;
Streams of mercy, never ceasing,
Call for songs of loudest praise.
Teach me some melodious sonnet,
Sung by flaming tongues above;
Praise the mount! I'm fixed upon it,
Mount of Thy redeeming love.

Here I'll raise my Ebenezer;
Hither by Thy help I'm come;
And I hope, by Thy good pleasure,
Safely to arrive at home.
Jesus sought me when a stranger,
Wand'ring from the fold of God;
He, to rescue me from danger,
Interposed His precious blood.

Oh, to grace how great a debtor
Daily I'm constrained to be!
Let Thy goodness, like a fetter,
Bind my wand'ring heart to Thee.
Prone to wander, Lord, I feel it,
Prone to leave the God I love.
Here's my heart, O take and seal it,
Seal it for Thy courts above.

~ Robert Robinson, 1758

Chapter 9

ATTACHED AND ATTUNED

*For this reason a man will leave his father and mother
and be united to his wife, and the two will become one flesh.*
~ Ephesians 5:31a

Parents are important. Without them we wouldn't even be here. And without them, we wouldn't know how to be in relationship with one another. Therein lies the source of some of the problems we encounter in Romance.

Dad and Mom taught us more than we realize. Some of it wasn't so good ... as if we were not sinful enough on our own to cause relationship troubles. I know, right?

But do not despair! What was learned can be unlearned. None of that stuff is written in stone.

The Scientific Theory of Emotional Attachment

Dr. John Bowlby, a British psychiatrist, was among the early researchers in Attachment Theory, and he explored the impact of the mother-child relationship. He noticed that, in addition to their need to be fed and protected, children also have a need for very strong *emotional* bonds with their parents or caregivers.

He proposed that we come into this world with an *attachment system* that assures our survival and safety in relationship to significant caregivers. So whenever a baby is distressed, this attachment system motivates him or her to seek closeness to a safe person.

When someone has been consistently *available* and *responsive* to the baby's needs, negative emotions (e.g., anger, fear, sadness, hurt) naturally decrease. The child is soothed and begins to develop the capacity to self-soothe by simply recalling the feelings associated with being comforted by a loving caregiver.

Based on these memories, a child develops a "template" for relationships that includes the beliefs that are essential for secure emotional attachment:
>   (a) I am lovable, and
>   (b) I can depend on others to be loving toward me and to help meet my needs.

Secure Emotional Attachment

Subsequently, other researchers have tested these ideas and found that interactions between a child's temperament and the caregivers' responsiveness will result in more or less secure styles of attachment.

As stated previously, our early experiences provide us with both images and emotions that form the template that serves as a pattern for understanding how to form relationships and how dependable we can expect them to be.

We learn about ourselves in relation to others based on
>   (a) their availability and responsiveness to us, and
>   (b) how effective we are in getting others to respond to our needs.

Although later experience may change our beliefs about the security of our relationships, we most often seek out people who fit the template we already have. Generally speaking then, if we developed an insecure style of attachment during childhood, it will probably continue to haunt us throughout adulthood ... unless a later relationship (e.g., with a human being or even with God) is established that provides a series of new experiences that help us become emotionally secure.

Research continues in the field of Adult Attachment Theory, with new information and more intricately defined models being formulated in recent years. As noted, I prefer to use a particular model in my explanation of attachment because of its simplicity and elegance in explaining the way a couple creates a beautiful Romance, as well as in describing the various ways that things can sometimes go painfully wrong.

Your Attachment Style

Because you are created in the image of God, you came into this world with a need for relationship. Your deepest desire has always been for an intimate relationship with Him ... as well as with another Someone ... who wears skin.

Your current attachment style is simply the result of your life experiences to date. So if another human being has been available and responsive to your needs on a consistent basis, you're probably in pretty good shape for Romance.

However, many of us – myself included – have experienced significant hurt and pain in close relationships ... especially with the opposite sex. If that's you, you may be having a hard time creating and/or maintaining a healthy Romance. But that can all change ... *for the better!*

So if you are feeling insecure, just think of it as true for you just for now. Because the Truth is that you were designed with an innate desire and capacity to form secure emotional attachments. How cool is that? Pretty darn.

Self-Assessment

You can assess your own emotional attachment security in a variety of ways, but one of the easiest is to take a look at what happens when you feel stressed out. How you handle stress (and express yourself) involves both your feelings and your actions.

We all get a bit anxious when we're under stress ... some more so than others, of course. Whenever you experience anxiety (worry, concern, fear, frustration, feeling trapped or stuck), then your ability to communicate is also affected.

You've also learned what actions to take when you're stressed. Are you someone who seeks out other people to help you with your stress? Or do you pull away from others and try to handle your stress on your own?

Secure Emotional Attachment

Securely attached men and women still experience anxiety, but at lower levels. When they're worried or concerned about something – inside or outside of the relationship – they seek out their partners to help them talk things through. After their talk, they feel less worried. If that sounds like you, you are probably more emotionally secure.

A securely attached man feels confident taking the lead in the Dance of Romance. That's not to say that he never has doubts or anxieties. However, when he does, he talks to his partner about it. He's learned that it's okay to be vulnerable with her – that she is a safe person for him. He knows that she will be available and responsive to his needs.

She never shames him or makes him feel bad about himself, but instead knows how to comfort him without making him feel like a little boy in the process. This can get a little tricky for women who don't really understand the differences between men and women in this regard. (We'll cover that in *Part 5: The Wonder of a Man.*)

A securely attached woman feels safe following her partner in the Dance. She trusts him and is confident that he has her best interest in mind ... that he won't drag her around like she's a rag doll ... or leave her standing there all alone.

She also trusts that he is paying very close attention to God's guidance, as well as close attention to her needs and desires. She knows he's open to her input and her feedback. It's not that he always does whatever she says; it's just that he is always willing to listen to her ideas.

She respects his developing leadership abilities, asks him for what she needs when she feels anxious, and can rest secure in his arms as he choreographs their Dance of Romance.

Insecure Emotional Attachment

As I mentioned, not all of us arrived at adulthood with a secure attachment style. The style you currently have could be Preoccupied, Fearful Avoidant, or Dismissing. Each has its own distinctive set of problems in Romance.

Preoccupied Attachment is characterized by a negative view of yourself (I'm *not* okay) and a positive view of the other person (you *are* okay). If that's you, you feel highly anxious in relationships, show a high level of dependence on others, and may invest significant energy in relationships that may not necessarily be in your best interest to maintain.

Someone with a Preoccupied Attachment style has difficulty loving, trusting, and respecting a partner in Romance, and might appear to be controlling or dominating. If that's you, then the greater your anxiety becomes, the more likely that you will appear to be angry, demanding, and/or critical.

Fearful Avoidant Attachment is characterized by negative views of both yourself and the other person (*neither* of us is okay). If that's you, you probably avoid getting too close to others because you're fearful of your own vulnerability.

You anticipate that others will be hurtful and may actually believe that you don't deserve to be treated well due to your perceived shortcomings. Although you may secretly desire Romance, you aren't likely to take that risk because you're afraid of looking bad, feeling rejected, or being criticized.

Although *Dismissing Attachment* is also characterized by social/relational avoidance, the interpersonal dynamics are quite different from those of Fearful Avoidant Attachment. If you have a Dismissing Attachment style, you probably have a more-or-less positive view of yourself (I *am* okay) and a negative view of others (You're *not* okay).

You see little, if any, value in intimacy and are consequently counter-dependent in your relationships. That is, you will often choose independence and autonomy over relational interdependence. In other words, you don't care much for Romance. At best, you think it's too much bother ... and at worst, it's just plain silly.

And there you have it. Many of us can identify a multitude of ways to make sure our relationships *don't* work. However, we're going to invest our energy on what actually *does* work. What works is very simple: being *available* and *responsive* to our partners "in the here-and-now," and caring about how our actions might affect others – especially the person we love most in this world.

So what does that look like?

For the most part, I think I'm getting pretty good at being *available* and *responsive* to my partner. Although I've become an "expert" on the psychology of men and relationships, the Lord teaches me more about both topics every day.

Once during a dance lesson, Fred and I were demonstrating the "swing" step, and he was telling the men how to make it enjoyable for the woman. He said, "Guys, you just pay attention to how your sweetie's body is responding to the music and to you, and then you match her."

Huh? For years I'd been telling women that they need to follow their guy – to match him. So I was more than a little taken aback by his verbal instructions.

I looked up at him and spontaneously proclaimed, "You're matching *me*? I thought I was matching *you!*"

He just smiled and replied, "We're matching each other."

Now I ask you, "How sweet is that?" A perfect way to play out Ephesians 5:21 – right in the middle of a dance lesson!

As couples, we must learn to pay attention to one another's needs and to be responsive to one another in light of the unique design and purpose given to us by Our Creator. Remember it was Christ who announced the revolutionary idea that husbands and wives are equal before Heaven, at the same time recognizing specific roles for each.

So if we want to build a Healthy Romance together, we need a more complete understanding of our respective biological differences, as well as differences in how we were nurtured. (That's what's coming up in *Parts 4 and 5*.)

In the mean time, let's take a look at some marital research. Over the years, unhappy couples have been able to create limitless possibilities for their unhappiness. Since that's not what we want to create, we'll want to concentrate most on learning to identify the characteristics of Happy Couples.

Blessed Be the Tie That Binds

Blest be the tie that binds
Our hearts in Christian love;
The fellowship of kindred minds
Is like to that above.

Before our Father's throne,
We pour our ardent prayers;
Our fears, our hopes, our aims are one,
Our comforts, and our cares.

We share our mutual woes,
Our mutual burdens bear;
And often for each other flows
The sympathizing tear.

When we asunder part,
It gives us inward pain;
But we shall still be joined in heart,
And hope to meet again.

~ John Fawcett, 1782

SIMPLE FACTS ABOUT MARRIAGE

He who finds a wife finds what is good,
and receives favor from the Lord.
~ Proverbs 18:22

You remember what happened in The Big Inning? The Lord said it wasn't good for the man to be alone, so He made a woman for him. He put Adam to sleep, took one of his ribs, and used it to make a woman. Then He brought the woman to her husband, who said of her,

This is now bone of my bones and flesh of my flesh;
she shall be called 'woman,' for she was taken out of man.
For this reason a man will leave his father and mother
and be united to his wife, and they will become one flesh.
~ Genesis 2:18-24

And They Lived Happily Ever After!

Not always, of course. But when they marry, both men and women are hoping to find their own Happily Ever After. No couple plans their wedding hoping to contribute to the divorce statistics. But it happens. Far too often.

We already know that the First Marriage wasn't always a Garden-of-Eden experience, right? The first couple had their share of problems, and contemporary couples do, too.

It doesn't take long for couples to figure out that Marriage is challenging, if not down right difficult at times. In fact, the number one reason people seek the help of a counselor is due to distress in a close relationship. Although marital difficulty doesn't always lead to divorce, it's good to know how to recognize the warning signs.

Dr. John Gottman, a major contributor to the field of marital research, has been studying couple relationships for more than 30 years in his Seattle clinic. So first, let's look as some characteristics of Happy Couples.

Happy couples respond positively to one another.

Partners continually make *bids* for one another's attention, closeness, and reassurance. They do so through comments, questions, and gestures. Those who are in more successful marriages will respond positively to their partner's bids at least 86% of the time. (FYI, my personal goal is 96-98%!)

Through their positive words and their positive actions, partners will invite more connection. They make the choice to communicate – with or without words – the feelings that "You matter to me," and "I want to connect with you, too."

Interesting Fact: Among successful couples, partners make at least 20 (yes, twenty) positive remarks for each (one) negative remark!

And happy couples argue.

What's important is how you go about it. Among couples with lasting marriages ...

1. About 80% of complaints came from wives. However, women raised issues gently and brought them up sooner rather than later.
2. Husbands were willing to be influenced by their wives and to change their behavior. Men didn't

simply do as their women said, but they were willing to consider their wives' input.

3. Neither spouse became upset enough with one another to raise their heart rates above 95 beats per minute. That would be a signal of the beginning of a fight-flight-or-freeze response.
4. They didn't escalate their arguments, but used humor, reassurance, and distraction to help ease the tension when it arose.
5. In fact, successful couples made at least 5 positive remarks or gestures for every negative during an argument. (Remember, when they weren't arguing, the ratio was about 20 to 1).

Now let's take a quick look at what factors predict divorce.

1. In an unhappy marriage, partners still make many bids for attention, closeness, or reassurance. However, they only respond positively to one another's bids 33% of the time.
2. Wives raise issues harshly and tend to make generalized statements, such as "You never ...," "You always ...," or "What's wrong with you?"
3. Unhappy husbands get upset more easily (as indicated by heart rate, breathing, etc.) during arguments and have a harder time calming down. As a result, they tend to shut down, become a stone wall, or withdraw from their wives.
4. Sometimes, wives shut down and/or withdraw from their husbands. It is particularly disastrous if the wife is the one to withdraw.
5. In short, when arguments start with a harsh comment, 94% of the time they only get worse!

Remember your need to be Securely Attached!

How well couples fare will depend greatly on the security of their attachment to one another. In other words, the bottom line for both men and women is the answer to the question,

"Will you be there when I need you?"

Throughout life, both men and women need someone who is *available* (will you be there) and *responsive* (when I need you). In fact, a secure emotional attachment is absolutely essential for your spiritual, physical, and mental well-being!

Re-establishing God's Created Order

As we'll discover, needs and purposes are a bit different for each sex. So we'll explore that in *Parts 4 and 5*. We need to make sure we have a crystal clear picture of the beauty of God's created order – just exactly what Romance should look like for men and for women in the 21st Century.

When a man and a woman partner with the Holy Spirit in their Marriage, it becomes an amazing experience for both of them – something Better Than Eden!

But first, there's one very important question – one that I get asked a lot – and I want to answer it for you now.

Chapter 11

Couples Only Have One Problem

Now to the unmarried and the widows I say:
It is good for them to stay unmarried, as I do.
But if they cannot control themselves, they should marry,
for it is better to marry than to burn with passion.
~ 1 Corinthians 7:8-9

We can merely guess Paul's thoughts and feelings when he wrote *that* passage. Many scholars believe he believed Jesus would be returning soon, so was likely more concerned with preaching the Gospel than with things of this world.

However, his advice reminds me of an old nursery rhyme:

Needles and pins. Needles and pins.
When a man marries, his trouble begins.

Which also makes me wonder why parents felt the need to warn children of the woes of Marriage at so young an age! That never happened in my house.

Oh, wait! That's right. I do remember now. When each son reached puberty, I warned him, "Stay away from girls, son. They're nothing but trouble."

They didn't listen. But then again, I knew they wouldn't.

Are you a Hopeful Romantic?

You may already have figured it out – from my website or from my previous book – that I am officially certifiable as a Hopeful Romantic.

A Hopeful Romantic is defined as a man or woman who not only loves the idea of Love, but also lives in the Real World. They hold on to their Faith as they Embrace the Possibilities of finding True Love. They have an abiding Hope that they will find a Special Someone, or may have already found that Special Someone. A Hopeful Romantic has the ability to see the world optimistically because they know from experience that God is Good. Hopeful Romantics always take time to grow in their relationships, never rush into things, and trust The Lord … Who is the Original Hopeful Romantic!

Now that the proverbial cat's out of its proverbial bag (as if it were ever in there in the first place), I'm going to pause and tell you exactly what it is that I so love about romantic movies.

As you can imagine, my family and friends have always loved to razz me about my tendency to quote lines from a wide array of romantic movies, books, and even comic operas …

As Good As It Gets. Christmas in Connecticut. Cinderella.
The Cutting Edge. Dan in Real Life. Double Wedding. Emma.
Enchanted. Ever After. The Ghost and Mrs. Muir.
He Married His Wife. Hope Floats. Joe vs. the Volcano. The Kid.
Mad About Men. The Mask of Zorro. Miss Congeniality.
Once Upon a Mattress. Overboard. Pretty Woman.
Pride and Prejudice. The Princess Bride. The Runaway Bride.
Sabrina. Sense and Sensibility. The Shop Around the Corner.
Shall We Dance? Sleepless in Seattle. Something's Gotta Give.
Tangled. Utopia, Ltd. What Women Want. When Harry Met Sally.
Yeomen of the Guard. You've Got Mail.

Remember it all starts with the "meet cute" at the beginning. Ah, the excitement, hope, and joy of a new relationship!

Next, the boy wins the girl ... or at least gets her attention. Then he screws up ... or at least she thinks he did. And the rest is about getting her back. So we're set up from the beginning to believe they will get together and live happily ever after. That's the way love's meant to be, right?

Love, you done me wrong!

I watch the movie *White Christmas* at least a dozen times every Holiday Season. My favorite scene is Phil and Judy (Danny Kaye and Vera Ellen) performing *The Best Things Happen While You Dance.*

But theirs is the secondary romance of the movie, which is really about Bob and Betty (Bing Crosby and Rosemary Clooney). It's a classic story of boy meets girl, boy gets girl, boy loses girl, then tries to win her back.

As in most relationships (e.g., Phil and Judy's), Bob didn't have to lose his girl at all! But somebody screwed up. Betty thinks it's Bob, so she exits to the Carousel Club, where she sings how "Love" done her wrong.

Many people – mostly women – believe their relationships go sideways because the guy screwed up. Not always true!

Sometimes, it's the girl who's got it wrong.

Women make a lot of assumptions – filling in the blanks with thoughts that paint a negative picture. We usually do it because we're actually afraid from the beginning ... afraid that something *will* go wrong. So we're almost relieved when it does.

Then we can blame the guy. And that's so very wrong!

Going around in circles ...

Romance always comes with a test. Wrapped up in the wonder of Love, we try to protect our precious possession. In doing so, we begin tiptoeing around. Which will raise questions for our partner, of course. Soon they start to wonder about our actions ... or our motives ... or both. Questioning another's goodness – or at least their good intentions – will always lead us down the path to failure.

We miscommunicate and don't know how to untangle it all. We misinterpret. Jump to false conclusions. We "knew it was too good to be true" and begin to seriously doubt Love. We fail to believe the best and begin to assume the worst. We start guessing about everything ...

She loves me? She loves me not? Daisies don't tell.

Remembering past pain and disappointments, we withdraw ... or we attack. We start guessing – or asking our friends – what we should do next. It's like we can't see the forest for the trees. And we don't even realize it's our fear – and more particularly, our *defense* against feeling afraid – that keeps us from having everything we've been hoping to have in Love. So we erect walls that no one could possibly hope to scale. The ultimate in self-protection.

Remember this!

It's not your *fear* that ruins your relationships. The only problem couples ever have is ... *Defensiveness.*

If you struggle to create or maintain a Healthy Romance, you are probably afraid of being hurt or getting dumped. And instead of having a healthy conversation about your fear, you're defensive, building self-protecting walls that not only keep out what's potentially bad or hurtful, but also everything that's right and good for you. (Learn to have a healthy conversation about your fears in Chapter 25, "The Role of Emotions and Understanding the Stone Wall.")

Hiding from Your Creator

That's also what happens in our relationship with the Lord. We're excited when we first meet Him and suddenly realize how much He loves us. His love is so strong that He sent His Only Begotten Son to save us from our sins (John 3:16).

We're certain – at least at the beginning – that He's going to give us the perfect life. No more pain. No more worries. And no more troubles. Everything will be just as it should.

But life is difficult. And those hard times – if allowed to do their work in us – will build deeper relationships!

But then the enemy comes along to steal, kill, and destroy (John 10:10); and tries to make us believe that our hard times are because the Lord is not all that He claims to be for us. Of course, He walks with us on a path that will become rough at times, and He will always bring good to us.

However, the enemy tells us we must have it all now! And because we don't have life on our own terms, we assume the Lord has screwed up when it comes to us.

So we believe another lie and put up walls to keep out the Lord Himself? How crazy is that?

Why not focus on the Truth instead?

> *Be strong and courageous. Do not be afraid or terrified because of them, for the Lord your God goes with you; he will never leave you nor forsake you."*
> ~ Deuteronomy 31:6

> *"I have told you these things, so that in me you may have peace. In this world you will have trouble. But take heart! I have overcome the world."*
> ~ John 16:33

Love Lifted Me

I was sinking deep in sin, far from the peaceful shore,
Very deeply stained within, sinking to rise no more,
But the Master of the sea heard my despairing cry,
From the waters lifted me, now safe am I.

Love lifted me!
Love lifted me!
When nothing else could help,
Love lifted me!

All my heart to Him I give, ever to Him I'll cling,
In His blessed presence live, ever His praises sing,
Love so mighty and so true, merits my soul's best songs,
Faithful, loving service, too, to Him belongs.

Souls in danger, look above, Jesus completely saves,
He will lift you by His love, out of the angry waves.
He's the Master of the sea, billows His will obey,
He your Savior wants to be, be saved today.

~ James Rowe, 1912

Part 4
The Beauty of a Woman

UNDERSTANDING AND LOVE

Woman is creatively designed to follow, and her partner's *love* and *understanding* are essential if she is to follow well.

So why are we starting with the follower instead of the leader? Because without her, he's got no hope for becoming all that he could be.

It isn't good for the man to be alone, remember?

And you can't be a leader if no one is willing to follow you.

But isn't *she* where things went so wrong in The Big Inning?

Yep. And that's *exactly* why we're starting with her ... so we can begin to set things right again ... under the grace of Christ and the power of the Holy Spirit.

Psychologists haven't been able to explain women to men.

Remember Dr. Sigmund Freud? Despite all his work with women in exploring the possibilities of "a talking cure," rumor has it that he died still wondering what women want.

Actually, we're not that complicated, but poor Siggy didn't have anyone to translate for him. Now you're going to get the inside scoop! In the next few pages, I'll share with you what a woman wants and needs from a man that will invest her with an absolutely *irresistible* desire to follow him.

Now how cool is that? Way cool.

Most of us believe that women are more complicated than men, but we're not nearly as complicated as we may seem.

In fact, most problems men have with women can be solved using a minimum of words and energy.

Really? That's a relief!

You see, The Problem is *how you see the problem*. And the problem you think you see is probably not The Problem at all. Women have just been taught to communicate in a very different way than men were. Our sex is actually *required* to communicate in a *Secret Code* (e.g., going around in circles, using too many words, never getting to the point).

All she needs is you *understanding* and *love*. And all you really need to understand is that she's not a guy; she's a girl. And love her simply because of who she is. So in the next two chapters, I'll break the code for you so you can figure out what she needs and what she wants.

Because this section is written for men, it'll be brief. You guys like to get to the point. I love that about you.

* A Word of Encouragement: I'll be spending a lot of time helping women learn to be more straightforward in their communication with men. We'll all be a lot happier for it.

Chapter 12

NOT SO COMPLICATED

Women are simple. That's an overstatement, of course. However, we are not nearly so complicated as we usually seem ... especially to men. However, women are different from men by our very nature. It's how we were created. And men actually prefer that, yes?

In fact, guys, there's no one you would rather dance through life with than a girl. However, the very things that draw you to us are the very things that you find confusing. You've probably wondered with Professor Henry Higgins (*My Fair Lady*) why a woman can't be more like a man.

But that's not really what you want. You love the fact that she's emotionally sensitive and not as big or as strong as you are. But you're also confused that so much depends on how she *feels*. And she feels *a lot*.

And she can talk forever and ever and ever and never get to the point. She looks to you to solve problems for her ... sometimes. But just as often, she can get really angry when you try to solve her problems ... especially if her feelings are involved. Sheesh.

Another thing that you probably don't realize is just how differently she's been treated her entire life ... just because she's female. From the moment her parents found out she was a girl, she has been viewed as sweet and delicate.

For example, as a toddler, she got picked on by another child at the park, and her mom or dad moved in quickly to intervene. She was given lots of comfort, understanding, hugs and kisses, and reassurance that she was cared for. Her tears meant something – helping her communicate that something was wrong. She had verifiable evidence that she mattered. Childhood was a very different experience for her than it was for you.

She was probably trained to be a pleaser. At the very least, she learned that nice girls never come right out and ask for what they want, that they take turns, and that they must always consider how other people might be feeling. So she learned to use a very tentative language, which now to you seems vague at best and just plain crazy-making at its worst.

She knew another girl was her best friend because they shared secrets with one another. Unlike your childhood friendships that focused on shared activities among a whole gang of guys, two-by-two proved the best pattern for her. Add a third girl to the equation, and it was an emotional disaster waiting to happen. Sounds weird, huh?

As if the tearfulness and the vagueness and the secret-sharing aren't enough, the differences between male and female communication are extensive. You wouldn't think the same English words could hold such different meanings for two people brought up in the same culture, but they do.

For example, take Sean and Nicole. They decided to take a day trip from Newport Beach to Solvang one Saturday. They'd been on the road for a couple of hours when Nicole said, "Do you want to stop and get something to eat?"

"No," Sean replied and kept driving.

Nicole's feelings were immediately hurt. But why? She asked if he wanted to stop, and he merely answered her question. What's the problem with that?

The problem was that he hadn't answered the question she was really asking. If he knew the Secret Code, he would have known that what she said was her tentative (feminine) way of saying that she was hungry and asking him if he would stop for her. He would have known to counter with, "Sure. We can if you'd like. Are you hungry?"

Women may be tentative because they fear being labeled as "needy" – which is not a compliment. Yet another reason is that we want to please *you* first and foremost, which is the honest explanation for our seemingly wishy-washy reply to your question, "Where do you want to go for dinner?"

When she says, "I don't care. Wherever you want to go is fine with me," she's just trying not to sound demanding ... and trying to please you ... which actually has the opposite effect. And yes, I am going to tell the women to stop doing that to you. *Sigh.*

In sum, she's different from you in that ...
- so much depends on how she feels,
- she values conversation for conversation's sake,
- and much of her self-esteem depends on what she thinks you think of her.

Yes, your opinion actually matters more than anything. She was raised to be a pleaser, and you are the one person she wants to please the most.

And if you are like most men, you would like to make her happy ... if you only knew how. But she unknowingly sets you up to fail by not being specific enough. We're going to work on that one for you, too. I promise.

But first, let's talk about what she needs from you. And in order to do that we'll have to break the Secret Code ...

When Maiden Loves

When maiden loves, she sits and sighs,
She wanders to and fro;
Unbidden tear-drops fill her eyes,
And to all questions she replies,
With a sad "Heigh-ho!"
'Tis but a little word – "Heigh-ho!"
So soft, 'tis scarcely heard – "Heigh-ho!"
An idle breath, yet life and death
May hang upon a maid's "Heigh-ho!"

When maiden loves, she mopes apart,
As owl mopes on a tree;
Although she keenly feels the smart,
She cannot tell what ails her heart,
With its sad "Ah, me!"
'Tis but a foolish sigh – "Ah, me!"
Born but to droop and die – "Ah, me!"
Yet all the sense of eloquence
Lies hidden in a maid's "Ah, me!"

~ Sir William S. Gilbert, 1888

Chapter 13

DECODING A WOMAN

Women aren't nearly as complicated as men think they are. Honestly, pretty much everything she struggles with in your relationship – as even she would confess – fits into one of the following three categories:

1. You don't love and cherish me.
2. You don't think I'm pretty.
3. You don't value my feelings.

As promised, this will be a short chapter, filled with bullet points and what-to-do's. You'll get enough detail to get the idea. And if it's not enough, please let me know. I'll be happy to elaborate online at www.OCChristianCouples.com

Bullet Point #1: Love and cherish her.

The first thing a woman wants is to know is that she's more precious to you than anything else. No, she doesn't want to run your life. She wants to know – by the reliability of your words and actions – that she's always at the top. Her hope and prayer is that she runs a very close second to God.

You probably don't realize just how important your opinion is to her. Despite how it may seem, much her self-esteem depends on what she thinks you think of her. Not what you *actually* think of her, but what she *thinks* you think of her.

And she makes that determination based on your behavior – all you choose to do – or choose not do – in regard to her.

The good news is that cherishing her is actually much simpler than you realize, and it's something that you already have a natural desire to do: *Be her Hero.*

All men love to be Heroes, so it comes naturally to you to behave like a Knight in Shining Armor to every woman you meet – the little lady who can't reach the last can of Who Hash on the top shelf at the market, to the gal with the flat tire who can't figure out the air machine at the gas station, and even to your grandmother.

But as a romantic partner, you may have forgotten the importance of being Gallant – Chivalrous, Courteous, Polite, Gentlemanly, Thoughtful, Gracious, Suave – towards her, especially if it seems like she doesn't *appreciate you. (*I promise to work with her on this one for you, too.)

So if you want her to follow your lead, the first thing you'll need to do will be to put forth extra effort in helping her realize that you are, first and foremost, *Her* Knight – and that *she* is the One Lady that you cherish above all others.

I can't emphasize this enough. This part is absolutely *crucial* if she is – or if you want her to be – your wife and lover!

If you haven't been Gallant for a while, there's no way you can go into this expecting an immediate payoff. Winning her trust will take some time – that is, you will need to convince her that you're treating her well just because you love her, and that you are not trying to get something in return … like *sex. Whatever you do, remember that it is simply your *Gift* to her, then be sure to act accordingly.

> * *Be encouraged. Sex is essential for both of you, and we'll be talking about why in Chapter 26.*

Where to begin ...

Every girl knows that a Hero does simple, everyday things to make you feel special. He opens the door for you and allows you enter a room first. He pulls out a chair for you at the table. When you go to a restaurant – even if it is only to your local Subway Sandwich Shop – he asks what you would like, then places your order for you saying, "The lady will have ..." adding his own order last.

Very sweet and very, *very* irresistible.

He makes eye contact when you are talking, which clearly communicates that all he cares about at this moment is you. He looks into your eyes and derives great pleasure in just seeing you looking back at him. He gives you a hug ... not because he wants sex, but because he finds you so adorable. And if he wants to take it over the top, he'll ask you to dance with him!

A guy can't help but be a Hero to his Sweetie as he glides her around our Dance floor. It's essential that couples keep the fun in their friendship, and Vintage Dance is the perfect place!

Great melodies and easy to learn Dance steps.
And you don't have to spend a fortune to enjoy an evening of Style and Elegance when Two Hearts are beating – and Dancing together – in three-quarter time!

There are so many ways you can help keep your relationship alive and well through fun and friendship, so be creative.

Dance With Me

Relationship Workshops

Men enjoy a hearty breakfast as Dr. Debi explains everything they need to know about women ... in 90 minutes or less!

Ladies relax over a lovely luncheon, then enjoy the afternoon as Dr. Debi unravels the Mystery of Men.

Couples end the day with a laughter-filled evening that provides an unparalleled opportunity to practice what they've learned in our charming 19th Century Ballroom!

Victorian Dance is stylish, elegant, simple-to-learn, ... and very, very Romantic!

But honestly, guys, Dancing is the absolute best, even if you have two left feet. She will love you for your honest efforts, so why not give it a try?

Magic Decoder Ring: Seven Top Clues that tell you she needs to know – by your *actions* – she's loved and cherished:

1. She says she wished you still _____
   (*talked to one another, held hands, had fun together*).
2. She complains that you never take her out anymore.
3. She stops getting gussied up (dressed up or fancy).
4. You know you treat her differently than you used to.
5. You spend more time ____ing than you do with her.
6. You haven't taken her anywhere that would give her an excuse to get gussied up in more than six months.
7. You haven't felt like a Knight in Shining Armor since … well, you just can't remember when.

Be on the lookout for more clues that she's missing her own Knight in Shining Armor. And if you're not sure, start being Gallant anyway. Who says you need a clue to do that?

Bullet Point #2: Tell her she's pretty.

This point's the simplest one. Women spend a lot of time, energy, and money trying to look as just pretty as they can. And as she gets older, she'll start doubting that she could still be attractive to the opposite sex.

If she's already yours – or if you want her to be yours – you won't want some other guy beating your time! So tell her yourself that she's pretty and/or cute … *on a daily basis!*

Of course, you must be absolutely, positively sincere about whatever you say. Flattery is cheap and meaningless, and she'll see right through it.

Don't go there.

Trust me. It's simply not worth the price.

Magic Decoder Ring: Seven Top Clues that tell you she's unsure she's still attractive to you:

1. You never ask her to Dance.
2. You don't tell her she's pretty or cute.
3. You don't look into her eyes when she's talking.
4. You don't look at her longingly as you once did.
5. She says, "Notice anything new?" and you don't.
6. She complains that you're looking at other women.
7. You haven't asked her out on a date since ... well, you just can't remember when.

Be on the lookout for more clues that she's questioning her attractiveness. Then pay her a sincere compliment each and every day. But who says you need a clue to do that?

Bullet Point #3: Just say you are sorry.

A woman's feelings can get hurt very easily, especially by the man she loves. Her feelings are important, and she needs you to appreciate that about her. In fact, feelings are *primary* for most women. When our feelings get hurt, we go into defensive mode. And everyone knows the best defense is a good offense.

So we often look and sound angry when, in fact, our feelings have been hurt. At that point, we'll either withdraw or attack, depending on our emotional attachment style (See Chapter 9). Hurting her feelings is tantamount to Crushing Her Spirit. Nothing good can happen until Her Spirit has been revived. When you learn how to help her with that, you'll reap rewards beyond Your Wildest Dreams. And it only takes three steps:

1. Notice that you hurt her feelings. That means you have to be paying attention, right?
2. Then say, "I'm sorry" or "I'm sorry I hurt your feelings." (Note: Say nothing more. Say nothing less.)
3. If she's angry and/or yelling at you, you'll need to say it at a distance. If she is crying, move in close and hold her hand or put your arm around her. Or if you're not physically present, you can tell her you wish you were

there to hold her hand or to put your arm around her. That works almost as well because this is one of those cases where it's mostly the thought that counts.

This concept is so simple, yet often so very difficult for you guys to grasp. So much so that I frequently spend an entire couple's counseling session explaining it to a man who objects to the apology on the grounds that he's done nothing wrong. The story goes something like this …

She fixes his favorite dinner as a special surprise for him one evening. He gets tied up at work and doesn't to call to say he'll be later than usual. When he arrives home, he doesn't notice anything special. He hurts her feelings.

She's noticeably upset and may even use words to tell him so, which may sound to him like attacking, criticizing, or blaming. He tries to explain what happened, thinking this will make her less upset. However, she hears his words as defensiveness … that he's making excuses … and trying to minimize the impact of his actions upon her feelings.

It's really simple, guys. Her feelings were hurt … by you. She understands that sometimes you get tied up at your job, and she knows that it can be hard for you to call when you're dealing with a crisis at work. That's *not* what she needs you to apologize for. Not even close!

She *only* needs you to apologize for *hurting her feelings*.

Here are three bullet points for clarification:

- You are *only* apologizing <u>for hurting her feelings,</u> which you *did* do … whether you meant to or not.
- She's the only one who knows when she's hurt. So *never* say, "I'm sorry *if* I hurt your feelings." It's tantamount to telling her she is crazy. And despite what you might think, she's *not* crazy: She's a girl!
- You are *not* apologizing for staying late at work.

When I explain this to a man during a counseling session, he invariably looks at his partner and says, "Really? *That's* all you want? That would *work*?"

She says, "Yes, that's all I want."

And then he doesn't believe either one of us ... until he gives it a try. For once, she's actually telling him specifically what she needs from him in a given moment. If he's wise, he'll listen and give it his honest effort.

To ensure you don't miss this very important part of the equation, as you are telling her you are sorry, remember:

Anger = Away (as in "keep your distance")
Tears = Touch (as in "get close enough to comfort her")

How to Win Bonus Points

If your woman is having a bad day, take her hands in yours and pray for her ... out loud.

Speak words of blessing over her, using Scripture to remind her just how much The Lord loves her.

It will be a life-changing moment for you both.

Were I Thy Bride

Were I thy bride,
Then all the world beside
Were not too wide
To hold my wealth of love – Were I thy bride!

Upon thy breast
My loving head would rest,
As on her nest
The tender turtle dove – Were I thy bride!

This heart of mine
Would be one heart with thine,
And in that shrine
Our happiness would dwell – Were I thy bride!

And all day long
Our lives should be a song:
No grief, no wrong
Should make my heart rebel – Were I thy bride!

The silvery flute,
The melancholy lute,
Were night-owl's hoot
To my low-whispered coo – Were I thy bride!

The skylark's trill
Were but discordance shrill
To the soft thrill
Of wooing as I'd woo – Were I thy bride

~ Sir William S. Gilbert, 1888

Chapter 14
WOMEN AND ANXIETY

The issue of women and anger is a very confusing one for a lot of men. Yes, I just said "anger."

I know the title of this chapter is "Women and Anxiety," but when a man sees his woman upset, all he can tell for sure is that she's angry. After all, that's exactly what he sees and hears and feels. Typically, he doesn't think to look past her anger for what might be lurking beneath the surface.

Most of the time, what looks like intense anger, is actually panic. A woman often freaks out when her man freezes up. She's probably thinking: "You're not listening to what I'm saying. You just don't get how much this means to me. You don't have any respect me or my feelings. You don't care."

She feels like she's drowning, and that her man doesn't care that she's drowning. He could be her rescuer … if he only knew that's what was going on. But he doesn't.

So he ends up feeling like he's drowning himself … caught up in the swirling intensity of her emotions. That is, he may feel very much like someone who's trying to save a drowning person, and ends up being pulled under the water himself by the panic by the very person he's trying to rescue. That's really what's going on in those moments.

I know it's next to impossible – when you're the victim of a woman's verbal attack – to think she's afraid of something. It wouldn't be *any* man's first thought.

But, more than likely, she's not merely angry. When you can recognize her fear and *think* about finding out why she's afraid, it could be a very, very helpful *thought* to have.

A Man's Anger

A woman also has a really hard time when her man is angry. And it really doesn't matter if it's he's angry at her or something else. Even if he's feeling generally frustrated with life, his behavior can evoke anxiety in her. It's really very, very scary for a woman to be around any angry man.

If she's your woman, her immediate thought is, "What's wrong? Did *I* do something? Why are you so mad at *me*?"

Yes, it could be the other drivers who are frustrating you. Or it could be something at work. Maybe you don't feel well ... or whatever. But if it comes across as anger, your woman will still become terrified.

When women are terrified, they come across as angry. And when men are angry, it terrifies women. So we end up with a vicious cycle of anxiety and negative interactions.

The Truth About Women and Anxiety

The vast majority of women deal with anxiety on a daily basis. We're anxious about a lot of things, especially when it comes to men. Here are a few examples that apply to most women:

Her physical safety. Ask her, "When was the last time you were afraid for your physical safety?" You'll probably be surprised by her answer. More than likely, it was sometime within the last twenty-four hours.

Women constantly scan the environment for danger, especially if they have to be out after dark without you for protection. We look for danger so automatically that we can't imagine that you men don't do the same. We don't realize that you're confident you can protect yourself if you need to do so. However, we must plan our defense, which usually involves (a) escape and/or (b) calling for help.

Displeasing you. Women are taught from early childhood to be pleasers ... something that intensifies with the onset of that wonderful phenomenon known as *puberty* ... mostly because we have been led to believe that there is a verifiable shortage of desirable men. Historically, that has been true. And it feels even more true to a woman who is unsure of herself to begin with.

We fear if we are displeasing, you'll reject or abandon us. Sometimes a woman may appear overly confident. But that actually may be her Fear in Disguise and can come across as "She doesn't really care about me."

When in doubt, assume that she fears displeasing you.

Feeling unimportant. For the last several years running, the most popular post on our *Psychology of Men* blog has been "Why Do Men Stonewall?" Stonewalling is withdrawing or refusing to respond to your partner. For you, it may be a response to your own confusion or feeling overwhelmed when she's upset. Or you may just try to stay calm in the hope that she will also calm down.

However, when you stay calm, it feels like you're just being nonresponsive to her, which only serves to make her even more anxious. The message your nonverbal behavior sends is that you simply don't care that she's upset. In reality, it's counter-productive, and actually will increase her anxiety and frustration, propelling you both into the same negative cycle that you are trying so hard to avoid.

It goes something like this, doesn't it? She begins a conversation with something that sounds harsh – something that feels like it came out of the blue. She's actually tapping on the door, trying to make contact with you.

When you fail to respond, she assumes you didn't hear her, so she talks a little louder. Now she's knocking on the door wondering if you are even in there.

Your heart races as you think, "Here we go again. This is not going to be good." You try even harder to remain calm, hoping that she'll settle down.

You might even try talking firmly or "logically" to try to calm her ... which only feels condescending to her. Shaming is not exactly sending her the message that she can depend on you to be there for her when she needs you.

If she wasn't really angry before this, she is now. Her feelings are seriously hurt, and she's in defensive mode (please refer to Bullet Point #3). She's now coming through the door with a two-ton wrecking ball, and she's determined that you *will* hear her out.

To you, she's in some sort of crazy rage, and you may begin to wonder if she has serious mental health issues. So you'll have a difficult time realizing that, underneath her anger, is a huge backlog of fear.

She may have a difficult time recalling her original feelings, too. However, your best bet is always that she started the whole conversation at least a little worried that her concerns would be totally unimportant to you – based on verifiable evidence from any stone walls you've erected previously.

I have to tell you that I really do understand why you guys do this so often and so automatically. It makes total sense to me, and I do my best to educate the gals about how their emotions impact you.

However, you must understand what happens for her as well. Basically, when a woman is emotionally flooded, and her partner shuts down during a disagreement, she's most likely to say she feels:

abandoned	isolated	shut out
blown off	lonely	undesirable
dismissed	pushed away	unloved
frustrated	rejected	unwanted

Well, *that* was not what you were going for, right? You only wanted her to be reasonable – to stop making such a big issue out of whatever it was – or at least not to attack, blame, or criticize you in the process.

There *is* hope for redirecting this scenario, and the best place to start is with Bullet Point #3. If it happens a lot, you may want to find a good couple's counselor – one who gets where *you* are coming from, as well as *her* position.

The Bottom Line

Without a doubt, this isn't a comprehensive explanation of all women ... or even of *your* woman. But if you apply these Basic Principles in your relationship, you *will* see a change. Remember, she may not trust you at first. In fact, you can count on a least some skepticism. If things have been rocky for a while, she may wonder what's happening at best and may suspect you're trying to manipulate her or that you're "up to no good" at the worst.

Just remember that a woman often worries about her physical safety, as well as whether or not she is displeasing and/or unimportant to the man she loves. But that's not all. We have other fears, too.

Song of Songs

I arose to open for my beloved,
and my hands dripped with myrrh,
my fingers with flowing myrrh,
on the handles of the bolt.

I opened for my beloved,
but my beloved had left; he was gone.

My heart sank at his departure.
I looked for him but did not find him.
I called him but he did not answer.

~ Song of Solomon 5:5-6

Chapter 15

A MAN'S LEADERSHIP

Do you know what a woman's Number One Fear is?

A major fear that remains unspoken for many a Christian woman is that her man will not be the Spiritual Leader of their family. So she takes over, and she doesn't do it well. Although it's better for the man to take the lead, especially with the children, she reasons that a *female* Spiritual Leader is better than *no* Spiritual Leader.

However, once she's taken on that role – before or after marriage – it'll be very difficult for you to step up to the plate. So *please* be the leader, in every sense of the word. Don't live life under the curse anymore!

> *The most important task you have been assigned is to continually direct and redirect your loved ones toward Christ. Only He can meet all their needs ... and yours!*

Leadership is your responsibility. You were designed to take the lead. God created you with all that it takes right there inside of you. It's a learning process, for sure, and no man comes into this life knowing how to lead. So get all the support you can.

As a husband, you'll be held responsible before God for your family. God knew it was Eve who took the first bite of the apple, but He came looking for Adam. You can believe me when I say I know that women can be difficult to love sometimes. I'm one of them, remember?

Remember the Dance

A man and a woman dancing together in three-quarter time is the best metaphor for – and experience of – Romance.

He takes the lead. She follows. He guides and protects her. She influences him, even as she admires him ... and makes him look good to anyone who's watching.

In one of my favorite waltz videos, so many couples are on the dance floor it's hard to imagine how they keep twirling around without crashing into one another. That is, unless you realize that each pair has only one leader.

The man's job is to protect his partner from other couples on the floor, and to guide her steps as they swish and swirl in time to the music. If the woman criticizes what he's doing or starts to pull him in a different direction, it'll be virtually impossible for him to take responsibility for the dance.

As Christian women, most of us have been taught that the man is to be the leader in the family. But in reality, women have been running the show for a long time now. Yes, she knows she can make it through life without you.

But can she really live the life she desires?

Yes, she would survive. But in taking charge, she misses the beauty of what God intends your relationship to be. She not only makes it impossible for you to lead, but she denies what her heart and yours are both longing for.

Three Things She Needs From You As Her Leader

She needs you to protect her, to guide her, and to hold her. And as her leader, you are designed by God to do just that!

Please Protect Me

As a man, you were designed to protect her. It's a fact of life that men are bigger and stronger than women. And you guys have this particularly wonderful quality about you: You have much, much, much high testosterone levels. A woman's body produces testosterone, too, but far, far less of it than a man does ... without even giving it so much as a first or a second thought.

However, this very fact can make her afraid of you. When she feels intimidated or threatened by a man, she will use the only surefire weapon she has: her words.

And given that you are sensitive to her, her words usually work to "cut you down to size." Not a bad thing if you were her enemy. But if you're her partner in life, that will make it next to impossible for you to be able to protect her.

Please Guide Me

Okay, this one may be difficult for your woman to admit. But she really wishes someone knew the answers. And she really wishes it was you who knew. She loves it when you solve a problem for her ... and you do, too! Your brain was made to solve problems, so she's actually helping you fulfill your purpose in life when she accepts your guidance. So it's very satisfying for you when you win in this way ... finding a workable solution that makes life better for her.

However, guys often get a bum rap for trying to solve a gal's problems for her ... because sometimes she just wants him to listen. So if that's what you want, all you have to do is tell him that up front.

Most men are more than happy to provide whatever will make you happy, but you must be specific about what you want because they can't think like a woman ... at all!

Please Hold Me

This one is probably the most important of the three things a woman desires from the man she loves. And it happens so naturally while you dance. (Maybe that's the reason I love waltzing so much!) Women not only want to be touched, but they want to be held ... lovingly, caringly, respectfully. Research shows that being held by someone you love will dramatically reduce anxiety in a matter of minutes! We've all seen an anxious toddler benefit from being scooped up and held by a loving parent. As adults, we're no different. We all need to be held sometimes. And women need it every day!

We're vulnerable creatures, but we often don't feel safe enough to admit it. We often get a bum rap by being called "needy" ... especially by men. And we hate that. So we'd rather not say how we're feeling ... or ask to be comforted, reassured, held.

And that's really, really sad. Because a man loves and receives measurable emotional and psychological benefits from holding the woman he cares for. If he only knew that's what you needed.

Most of the time, he just thinks he's screwed something up and that you would like to have him beheaded. We'll find out why that is in *Part 5: The Wonder of a Man.*

Chapter 16

LEARNING TO FOLLOW

A few years ago, I asked students in my undergraduate psychology classes if – generally speaking – they thought it would be acceptable behavior for a girl to ask a boy out on a date. The women said yes ... and so did the men ... sort of.

Further discussion revealed that, although they would find it flattering that a girl was interested in them, almost all the men said they'd feel at least a little uncomfortable with that ... and they'd rather be the one to do the asking. Go figure.

Without a doubt, women can be a great leaders. However, Romance is not the best place to demonstrate those abilities. Instead, this is the one place in the world where we get to relax and enjoy being a girl ... for the most part.

Being in relationship with a member of the opposite sex can be fun ... challenging ... and hard work. And the benefits of loving a godly man by far outweigh the effort it takes to understand him. We'll be unraveling the mystery of the male in *Part 5: The Wonder of a Man*.

As a Hopeful Romantic, I believe that having someone to love who actually loves you back is worth more than anything else we will ever have or do in this life.

Submission in the 21st Century

Submission gets a bum rap. But it isn't at all like it might seem, as you'll see in *Part 7: Submission in the 21st Century*. For our purposes here, just think of submission simply as *trust* and *respect*. It goes like this ...

- Demonstrate unparalleled respect for him as a man.
- Trust him – and the Lord – to lead you.
- Love him just as he is.
- Long for all the best of what God has for him.
- Make him look good to others.
- And give him immediate affirmation whenever you believe he's on the right track.

As you pray for him – and I believe this should happen continually (1 Thessalonians 5:17) – it will be very helpful for you to keep these particular verses in mind:

> *He who finds a wife finds what is good*
> *and receives favor from the lord.*
> ~ Proverbs 18:22

> *She brings him good, not harm,*
> *all the days of her life.*
> ~ Proverbs 31:12

The Benefits of Partnering With a Godly Man

Always remember that you were created for him, not the other way around. Yes, I know this isn't a very popular statement, but I firmly believe it's a Fact of Life. Men don't do well without us (Genesis 2).

But when you try to turn a man into what you want him to be ... as though he were created for your benefit ... nothing good will come of it. I've never seen a situation wherein the woman called all the shots, and the relationship was a lasting and happy one for both partners.

Yes, he needs to listen to you. But if he does everything you tell him to do, you've got a serious problem on your hands.

However, you'll reap immeasurable benefits as you become the wife he needs you to be.

- You'll be positively, absolutely irresistible to him.
- He'll joyfully protect you and provide for you, hold you and guide you.
- He'll believe in you and be Your Biggest Fan.
- He'll be proud of you when you do well, and right there for you when you need him.
- He'll love you, care for you, and respect you.

What more could a woman ask for than that?

Song of Songs

Like an apple tree among the trees of the forest
is my beloved among the young men.
I delight to sit in his shade,
and his fruit is sweet to my taste.

Let him lead me to the banquet hall,
and let his banner over me be love.

Strengthen me with raisins,
refresh me with apples,
for I am faint with love.

His left arm is under my head,
and his right arm embraces me.

~ Song of Solomon 2:3-6

Part 5
The Wonder of a Man

TRUST AND RESPECT

You'll notice that Part 5 is longer than Part 4 because men aren't as simple as they believe they are. And because women have strong beliefs about men – mostly false beliefs that are frequently perpetuated by the men themselves.

Another equally important reason this section is longer is because I believe that when men get the essentials they need from us to be successful Leaders in the Dance of Romance, they will naturally respond to us just the way we want and need them to respond. I've seen it happen over and over.

But women don't understand how a man thinks, what he feels, and why he behaves the way he does. Men often seem complicated because women have no explanation for them ... at least not an explanation that he offers.

So women are confused about men. And men are confused about themselves ... sometimes. But mostly, they operate by Very Different Rules than women do. What is obvious to a man can be utterly confusing to a woman. So our goal is to end – or at least begin to end – her confusion about men.

You may be surprised to learn that nature and nurture play out in male development in ways that simply don't go that way for women. Some Really *Big* Differences that make his behavior confusing – and him very desirable! He has very good reasons for the way he is. And once you understand the Truth about his template, you'll develop the capacity for a greater appreciation for who he is as a man.

We'll explore the "Stages of a Man's Life," which are very different than they are for a woman. His age and where he is in the process of life will provide even more explanation and understanding of why he does things the way he does. I promise, he *will* make sense to you ... at last!

Beyond that, you'll also want to know what he needs from you ... mostly because he never asks for what he needs. And there's a good reason for that, too!

But mostly it's about trust and respect.

I Have a Song to Sing

I have a song to sing, O!
SHE: Sing me your song, O!
It is sung to the moon
By a love-lorn loon,
Who fled from the mocking throng, O!
It's a song of a merryman, moping mum,
Whose soul was sad, and whose glance was glum,
Who sipped no sup, and who craved no crumb,
As he sighed for the love of a ladye.

Heighdy! heighdy!
Misery me – lack-a-day-dee!
He sipped no sup, and he craved no crumb,
As he sighed for the love of a ladye!

I have a song to sing, O!
HE: Sing me your song, O!
It is sung with the ring
Of the songs maids sing
Who love with a love life-long, O!
It's the song of a merrymaid, peerly proud,
Who loved a lord, and who laughed aloud
At the moan of the merryman, moping mum,
Whose soul was sad, and whose glance was glum,
Who sipped no sup, and who craved no crumb,
As he sighed for the love of a ladye!

Heighdy! heighdy! Misery me – lack-a-day-dee!
He sipped no sup, and he craved no crumb,
As he sighed for the love of a ladye!

~ Sir William S. Gilbert, 1888

Chapter 17

NOT REALLY THAT SIMPLE

A few years ago, a young couple came into my office for their first session of marriage counseling, and right away I could tell that the husband didn't want to be there. He took one look at me, and by the expression on his face, I could just imagine what he was thinking.

"Great. Just great. Our last therapist was a man, and he seemed pretty good, but my wife didn't think he was helpful. So now we're going to talk to a *female* counselor? Oh, brother! Here we go again. Only this time, I'm going to get it in stereo. Ok, suck it up, buddy, and get ready to go three rounds with not one, but *two* women hammering away at you for the next 45 minutes. And at the end of it, you get to write the woman a check. I'm such a lucky guy."

His wife appeared a little anxious – and a lot frustrated. She began with a very intense explanation, even before they were seated. "He never talks to me. In fact, all I get is the cold shoulder. Whenever I try to discuss an issue, he tunes me out! He just sits there, staring at the TV. Sometimes he gets up and storms out of the room … without saying a word! He's just so insensitive. I don't see how this marriage will ever work if he's not willing to talk about things. I'm ready to give up. I've tried everything I can think of to get him involved with the family. How can he *not care* about his own wife and family?"

I listened patiently to her lament, and out of the corner of my eye, I could see her husband slowly sinking into his end of the sofa.

I nodded understandingly at his wife, then said, "I can see how hard you're working at this – trying to make your marriage work – and how distressed you are. This is really, really hard for you."

Anticipating my alliance, she sat up straighter and listened intently as I joined her in her frustration. "Being in a painful relationship is incredibly difficult, I know. And you know what else? ... We've actually been lied to."

Her husband continued to sink a bit deeper, while a slight smile stole across his wife's face as she waited for more confirmation of what she thought she already knew – that she was right, and he was wrong.

"Yes," I continued. "We've been lied to. We've been led to believe that men are insensitive jerks. That they're not in touch with their emotions – if they even have any. That they just don't get it. It's like the elevator doesn't stop on that floor. But the truth is ... men are actually *more* sensitive than women."

The wife tipped her head sideways, like a bright-eyed cocker spaniel who couldn't believe her ears. I imagined she thought, "What? This can't be right! This woman is *not* going to be helpful. She obviously doesn't know *anything* about men!"

Anticipating her confusion, I supported my statement with some research findings, and she appeared to be a little bit more interested. I imagined she was thinking, "Well, maybe she does know a *little* something about men. Maybe she *can* fix my husband ... or at least get him to talk to me!"

At the other end of the sofa, her husband seemed to breathe a sigh of relief, sat up a little straighter, and almost smiled. If he had been more verbally inclined at that point, he might have said something like, "Hey, this woman gets us guys. This therapy stuff might actually work this time. Thank you, Lord! ... I just hope my wife pays real close attention."

Men Do Think About Their Relationships – A Lot!

As we will discover, most men process their thoughts internally – before they speak. They are taught to do so. Because they often don't share their thoughts with their partners, women erroneously assume men don't think about the future ... or devise a plan for getting their families from Point A to Point B. Nothing could be further from the truth!

According to author Gordon MacDonald, men have a lot of serious thoughts – about a lot of stuff.

> *Among all these thoughts are the private thoughts. They are the ones I hold on to most tightly for fear that, if exposed, they might show a side of me that almost no one knows or would understand: the side that includes thoughts of possibilities, failures, dreams, fears, desires, shame, beliefs, regrets, memories – both good and bad – and, well, the list goes on and on.* (p. xviii)

The Making of a Man: Nature and Nurture

Researchers and philosophers originally debated about the role of nature *versus* nurture in directing the process of human development. Findings have been inconsistent in terms of which is more powerful, our biology or our environment. Consequently, they sort of gave it all up and focused their studies on understanding the interactions between these primary two factors.

Because psychological experiments on human beings (as well as many animal experiments) are unethical, we are left to our observations of what exists naturally within the world – not unlike King Solomon. Without the benefit – or the risk – of studying cause-and-effect relationships, we can only recognize correlations among various factors and suggest probabilities.

The bottom line, then, is that we can only report what's likely to happen and conclude that we can't really know anything for sure. That is, in applying any research finding to real-life situations, we must admit that it all depends upon a multitude of factors. However, what we learn can be helpful in providing some probable – or at least plausible – explanations for why people are the way they are.

The same is true for the information shared here. Although something *probably* applies to most men, it may or may not apply to *your* man. Therefore, you are encouraged to summarize what you glean from this book and to ask your guy whether or not it fits him. At the very least, he will be flattered that you cared enough to ask. At the very best, you will have had an opportunity to learn more about him, and that is always a very, very good thing.

Nature: Men are more sensitive than women.

Researchers have found evidence that male infants are more emotional than female infants from birth until at least six to twelve months of age. Infant boys cry more frequently and intensely, coo and smile more often, and experience more rapid fluctuations in emotional states than do girls. However, by two years of age, there is already a noticeable reversal in verbal expression; and by six years of age, there is a noticeable difference in facial expression as well.

Furthermore, boys seem to have a natural tendency to express their feelings more through *action* than by talking about them. Whatever the reason, boys demonstrate an ability to avoid overt responses to emotion between four and six years of age – interestingly, about the time they usually enter kindergarten. (We'll explore some possible explanations for that in a moment.)

So fast forward to adulthood. Once they grow up, do men even *have* feelings anymore? Or have they simply been disconnected from their own emotions? Marital research conducted over the past several decades suggests that men really do have feelings – very strong ones – and that they are highly aware of each and every one of them.

In one particular study, couples volunteered to be observed interacting with one another. Video cameras recorded their spontaneous interactions, and researchers coded their behavior for analysis. Over time, the researchers began to notice that some participants tended to be very emotionally expressive (i.e., visibly and audibly upset or angry) during a disagreement, whereas their partners were not.

So the researchers devised a method to help determine what might be going on that wasn't directly observable. They asked the couples to sit in facing chairs and instructed them to discuss something about which they disagreed. Each person was connected to equipment that registered respiration and heart rate, as well as how much each wiggled in the chair. The data they collected showed that, although the seemingly non-responsive partners appeared to be totally cool and calm, their heart rates frequently rose above 95 beats per minute when things got tense.

Interesting, eh? It appears that cool and calm on the outside does not equal cool and calm on the inside.

I've found in counseling a wide range of couples, it's often the men who are most successful at *appearing* to maintain their composure. They may not be emotionally expressive, but their bodies sure are!

So it's no wonder that men often fail to respond verbally. They're probably too busy regulating their pounding hearts. After all, we know that one of the Rules of Manhood is "Never let 'em see you sweat."

And if men take action when they feel emotions … well a pounding heart *is* part of the *fight*-or-*flight* response. Which of those responses do you prefer when it comes to you?

So what about nurture?

Going back to Attachment Theory (Chapter 9), you'll recall that healthy human development relies heavily upon the processes of relationship, especially upon our primary need for emotional connection with someone who is *available* and *responsive* to our needs. However, boys typically experience relational trauma that girls rarely do. It usually goes something like this …

As a toddler, he got picked on by another kid at the park, and his mom or dad held back to see what he would do. When he came to report the offense, he was required to provide explanation. His tears were something shameful. Big boys don't cry, so stop whining and figure out what to do. He learned that he was on his own – that he would have to solve his own problems somehow. Childhood was a very different experience for him than it was for you.

He knew he had friends because of their shared activities. Unlike you and your best friend in childhood who shared intimate secrets, he was busy hanging out with a whole gang of guys who did stuff together. No secret-sharing.

And according to research psychologist Dr. William Pollack, every boy learns "The Boy Code" as a matter of course:

- *Be a Sturdy Oak*
  Whimpering, crying, complaining, or any sign of weakness is strictly forbidden.
- *Give 'Em Hell*
  Risk-taking behavior of a macho, invincible, sometimes violent, high-energy superman is encouraged.
- *Be the Big Wheel*
  Dominate others and refuse to let anyone know you actually feel like a failure or like life is out of control.
- *No Sissy Stuff Allowed*
  This last commandment is what Dr. Pollack believes prohibits boys from expressing any feelings or urges that might be viewed as feminine, such as dependence, warmth, empathy. Great, huh?

Where's mom?

Mom is usually our first relationship, and until a boy reaches about three years of age, his relationship with his mother is very similar to that of a girl with her mother. Then, sons and mothers begin to relate to each other in a different way than do daughters and mothers, and the vulnerable feelings that arise around this disconnection may have very profound implications for the rest of male relational development.

American culture in general supports this disconnection, which researchers refer to as *normative developmental trauma*, which a girl isn't required to experience. A boy is pressured to disconnect from his mother – usually through shaming by other boys and men. In addition, his mom is expected to support his turning away from her, even if she feels it is wrong to do so. He must be declared different from her, compares himself to others, tries to be unique, and feels bad when he is unsuccessful.

Perhaps as a consequence of her own misunderstanding of men, a boy's mom is usually the one to fit him with his first "gender straitjacket" through emotional shaping that begins at birth and continues throughout the life span. In the process of attachment and (frequently traumatic) separation, she actively (though often unwittingly) participates in the hardening process that shames boys into suppressing their empathic and vulnerable sides. One of the first things a mother wants to know is whether the child is a boy or a girl. As soon as she knows, the process begins.

Dr. Stephen Bergman also noted, "Often the boy is taught not to listen to his mother trying to maintain connection, or to listen with a certain suspicion, and if he does listen, not to respond to her." As a result, he may become paralyzed both emotionally and relationally by his own ambivalence – his intense longing for close emotional connection and the fear of his vulnerability at the same time. Very confusing and sad ... and very, very lonely.

At this point, he needs to identify with someone – ideally, with a caring, available father. However, his father may also be encouraging the mother-son disconnection, be recovering from his own relational trauma, and be unable to provide him with the empathic relationship he so desperately needs.

Consequently, the boy moves from a mother connection to a father *dis*connection. Rather than learning to maintain the emotional ties essential for development, he learns to disconnect from the process of relationship, and may never learn how to be emotionally close with another person.

Male Relational Dread

Thus, not having learned to deal with unpleasant emotions in relationship when he was a boy, a man may continue to feel intensely afraid of conflict, as well as connection. Bergman labeled this emotional experience using a highly descriptive term: *male relational dread*. A man's fear is characterized by a sense of inevitable, never-ending disaster and an expectation of immense and irreparable damage. And often the closer a man feels to a woman, the more intense his dread. He feels unsafe, guilty, incompetent, and ashamed in this uncharted territory.

Under the pressure of needing to fix things, he is overcome by an ever-increasing sense of dread. Although a man may want connection desperately, he may withdraw, strike out, tune out, change the subject, joke, make nice, or simply fall silent in an effort to deal with his anxiety.

Gordon MacDonald put it this way:

> Among the first private thoughts in the male are ones that center on the issue of feelings, which most of us are taught, should rarely, if ever, be acknowledged. The don't-cry-act-like-a-man message comes early in life. And a boy learns to master his tear ducts and force his face into an expression that would make a stoic proud. The feeling may be unbearable, *he thinks*, but there's no way I'm

doing to let you know it. *From that point forward in the male life feelings and emotions are increasingly stuffed somewhere. Fear, sadness, anxiety, smugness, anger, joy, loneliness, disappointment:* don't let them be seen, deep-six them, make them disappear, so far away, so deep, so buried that no one, even I, will ever know they were around. (p. xix)

It's indeed most unfortunate that many men have sufficient evidence from their own relationships with women that disconnection may actually be the better, safer way to go. Men – no doubt with good reason – do not trust women to let go of their false images of men, and to accept and appreciate their vulnerability as human beings.

However … the good news is that you have the power to change that experience for *your* man – starting today! Simply learn the Truth about how to be a *safe person* for him. And if you don't know what that looks like, find a knowledgeable counselor who can help you develop the understanding and skill required. You will both be the better for it.

My Hope Is Built

My hope is built on nothing less
Than Jesus' blood and righteousness;
I dare not trust the sweetest frame,
But wholly lean on Jesus' name.

On Christ, the solid Rock, I stand;
All other ground is sinking sand,
All other ground is sinking sand.

When darkness veils His lovely face,
I rest on His unchanging grace;
In every high and stormy gale,
My anchor holds within the veil.

His oath, His covenant, His blood
Support me in the whelming flood;
When all around my soul gives way,
He then is all my hope and stay.

When He shall come with trumpet sound,
Oh, may I then in Him be found;
Dressed in His righteousness alone,
Faultless to stand before the throne.

~ Edward Mote, 1834

 *Chapter 18*

CREATED WITH PURPOSE

For man did not come from woman, but woman from man;
neither was man created for woman, but woman for man.
~ 1 Corinthians 11:8-9

Man was created first. Then woman was created for man.
No, that's not a popular idea, but it's right there in the *Bible*.

If we back up to the very beginning, we see that men have
needed us from the start. Man was originally created with a
need for relationship – and God's answer was a woman.

> *The Lord God said, "It is not good for the man to be alone.*
> *I will make a helper suitable for him."*
~ Genesis 2:18

I like the way Pastor Mike Erre said it when he spoke at
Mariners Church in Irvine, California:

> *.... God created mankind in His Own Image. In the*
> *Image of God he created them. Male and female he created*
> *them .... And instead of it being good, it's very good ....*
> *The Bible begins with the fundamental, absolute, and*
> *unambiguous declaration of the equality between men*
> *women .... Both male and female are needed to reflect*
> *fully the image of God.*

> *Adam, flying solo through the animal kingdom ... God*
> *looks at him ... the Lord God said "It is not good for the*
> *man to be alone. I will make a helper suitable for him."*

Now in English, that sounds like, "Adam, you're very important, so you need an executive assistant" … or "You need someone to kind of clean up your mess." But the word helper … in Hebrew … it's a very strong word. It's actually used of God. God as a rescuer. So David will cry out to God, "O, God, You're my help. You're my strength." That's the same word, so you can translate this, "God looked at the man and saw that he needed a rescuer and provided woman."

Wow. That is *powerful*. What an important role we have to play! However, Pastor Mike went on to say that – as part of the curse noted in Genesis 3 – the woman's desire is to control, manage, and fix her husband. And that man will toil his life away. And they won't get along with one another. Remember Chapter 5?

However, we can now give thanks to the Lord for the hope we have through our faith in Jesus Christ, who sets things right again. In Ephesians 5, we learn that man is to *love* his wife and be willing to die for her … as Christ died for the Church. So far, that sounds like the Best Good Deal for Womankind. But that's not all there is to it. There's that part about the wife's submission, remember?

Clearly, we are created as partners. Essential partners in the work of the Kingdom of God. Through Christ, we are redeemed to fulfill the purpose for which we were created. Man is the Leader, and woman is the Follower. He's not a dictator, and she's not a silent, meaningless subject. More about that later …

Fortunately, when we get things back in their proper, Heavenly perspective, man has what he needs to do his job, to live out his life doing what God designed him to do. And man was created to be especially adept at four things (five, if you count parallel parking): protecting, providing, problem-solving, and pleasing. Yes, they all begin with the letter "p." That makes it easier to remember. How cool is that?

My Protector

Man protects instinctively. He protects the people he loves ... and sometimes even people he doesn't love ... and sometimes even people he loves – or doesn't love – who happen to be angry at him at the time.

Remember that he's more sensitive than a woman. Here's where this characteristic comes beautifully into play. His radar is alert for danger, and instead of analyzing his emotions, he takes action ... or gives you advice or tries to solve the problem. Which you often hate because you don't understand his intent. You erroneously believe he's trying to fix you just to shut you up.

Although that may be partially true (sorry for being so frank), it's mostly that a man doesn't like to see someone he loves suffering. He wants the pain to stop ... and to stop *now*. So he gives you advice. He's trying to protect you from further hurt. You can appreciate how really sweet that is of him ... when you understand why he's doing it.

However, his sensitivity can backfire in a heartbeat. If he feels like he is being attacked, blamed, or criticized, he will go on the defensive ... to protect *himself* rather than you.

And here is the really sad part: Most of the time, you have absolutely no clue that you might be saying or doing anything that could be even remotely related to attack, blame, or criticism.

This is where we need to understand the power of our language, and that words often hold very different meanings for a man than they do for a woman. So be sure to study carefully all of *Part 6: Life at the Tower of Babel* for help with communication.

Women have no less than a bazillion ways of telling men they don't measure up ... of taking away the power they have as men.

Here are just a few ways you might be communicating to him that you believe he is inadequate …

- You smirk or roll your eyes at him.
- You give him advice by saying something like:
  - Have you ever thought about … ?
  - Why don't you … ?
  - You should ….
- You talk about him to other people like he's not there.
- You laugh at him … when he's not trying to be funny.
- You blame him for whatever has just gone wrong, usually trying to make yourself look better.
- You correct or criticize him. This one is powerfully emasculating when you do it in front of other people.

A few months ago, I was waltzing with a friend at a very festive ball, when the couple ahead of us tripped, and the woman crashed onto the floor. Her partner, who was obviously concerned, responded immediately to help her to her feet. Her response? She glared at him, shaming him by her facial expression as well as her words. I'm still not sure for whom I felt more empathy: her for falling … or him for being yelled at in front of a ballroom full of his peers.

Note on Repairing a Disconnection: If he shuts you out when you're talking, stop and ask him what he heard you say. If he's honest with you, he'll tell you that it felt like an attack, blame, or criticism. And if he tells you that, believe him. It does *not* mean that's what you were *trying* to do. It just means that what you said got lost in translation, and you can try again … but use different words.

My Provider

Men love to provide for us. They see themselves primarily as Providers. In fact, there was a time when the primary determinant of a man's self-worth was how well he was able to provide for his family.

Maybe this is still that time.

You may have noticed that one of the first things a man tells someone is what he does for a living. His job, career, or profession is a major part of his identity. As old-fashioned as it sounds, most men still don't like being taken care of financially by a woman. It's not "a pride thing." It's just who they are … it's in their DNA.

As a 21st-Century woman, you probably believe that you can make it on your own. Unlike women before us (e.g., Elinor Dashwood in Jane Austen's *Sense and Sensibility*), most of us have ample opportunity for employment that fits our skills and training. There are other reasons we struggle financially, but the oppression we face in society is most certainly not what it used to be.

In fact, our social standing changed significantly in wartime … specifically during World War II. Our men were shipped overseas to fight, and we were left at home to run the country. When the guys returned home, we seemed to be saying to them, "What do we need *you* for?"

In this country, women have been running the show for a long time now. However, we also must realize the huge price we pay in doing so. Life isn't anything like it was in Jane Austen's day. Women have gained a tremendous amount of freedom, and rightly so. But have we gone too far in our quest for equality?

It's not just that we miss being protected, guided, and held by our man. It's also that, when women wear the pants, we lose something essential of who we are created to be … at all levels, intellectual, emotional, relational, physical, etc. In a word, we force ourselves to operate in "survival mode" and may never have the opportunity to thrive!

God designed women to be adaptable, which is a good thing. We have what it takes to rally when needed, but we can only do it for the short term. As a way of life, it can destroy us.

One of the ways men are better equipped to lead is because of their naturally higher testosterone levels. When women need to "step it up," they must rely on adrenaline, which is only a short-term solution – for any human being. If we rely on it long term, we destroy our bodies.

But that's not to say men don't run on adrenaline far too often as well. However, it's not their first resource in the drive to survive. If not psychosocially and emotionally emasculated – which may decrease testosterone levels – men have what it takes to go farther and faster than a woman does before their bodies begin to overuse their sympathetic nervous system for day-to-day survival.

In addition, there's actually a body of research that provides evidence that, in order for women to survive in business, they must have the ability take on masculine qualities ... especially when it comes to communication. In other words, they have to learn to walk and to talk and to act like a man, or they will fail in a Man's World.

And that isn't to say that women can't be good providers. Many of us have had to be the sole providers for our families. But women need to stay connected with and value their feminine qualities, and not try to become men. The converse is also true. Men need to be tender and sensitive and caring, but with the unique style that men have. We should not try to make our men into women.

My Problem-Solver

Men are wonderful Problem-solvers. Whenever you have a problem, he loves to be able to solve it for you. It brings him great satisfaction. It enhances his masculine sense of self. He loves it ... if you take his advice, that is.

But that isn't always what we're wanting, is it? Sometimes we just want him to listen and provide empathy. We can probably solve the problem by ourselves. If he jumps in and starts to tell us what we should do, we get angry ... usually because he hasn't heard the whole story.

And let's face it: We easily turn a simple story into a long and drawn out affair. It's just what we do.

For example, my friend was telling her husband about when she went to the mall to pick up some makeup she'd ordered from Macy's ... you know the kind that makes your skin feel like silk? It's the greatest creation ever! And as she was on her way to Macy's she walked past Pottery Barn, which was on the left side of the very busy courtyard, which at that very moment was filled to the brim with the most adorable gaggle of giggling children, playing on the indoor playground equipment with their mothers chatting cheerily nearby. The kids were so cute, and one little girl had on the most darling outfit. It had a great big strawberry applique on the front and the cutest little ruffles across her bottom. And her blonde curls bounced as she toddled around the courtyard with her friends. The scene reminded my friend of when her own kids had been toddlers, and about how much she misses them now that they've gone away to college. She paused just a moment watching the children and sighed, then immediately spied something in the window of Pottery Barn that drew her attention away from the playgroup. She'd been thinking about redecorating her bedroom, and there it was ... right there in the window of Pottery Barn ... the most beautiful Arista Palampore duvet cover and sham in a most charming delicate blue. Well, we all know that the most sought-after fabrics of 18th-Century France were those printed with indigo, a natural dye imported from the Far East and the New World. It was immediately apparent that this bedding would fully capture the exotic, romantic feel of those antique French textiles she'd been wanting – complete with a lush garden printed in soft color on an ivory ground. It would be perfect, especially since it was on sale, she reasoned. So she entered the store and struck up a conversation with another woman who was looking at the same display. They shared their decorating ideas, as well as the fact that their husbands saw no need for the change. And before they knew it, they realized they both went to the same college ... though several years apart. They ended up going for coffee, and next week they're all (yes, husbands included!) going to meet at the club for dinner. Isn't that amazing? (*Sigh.*)

My friend obviously – and obliviously – doesn't know this simple fact: that men listen in sentences (looking for a problem to solve or a purpose for relating the information), whereas women talk in paragraphs (sometimes volumes). My friend's poor husband was frustrated, and so was she.

As women, this kind of conversation is natural to us. That's how we connect with one another. Remember, when we were kids we knew someone was our best friend because we shared our secrets with one another. We do it with all our women friends, and they don't get annoyed. They counter with more stories, and we enjoy getting to know one another in that way.

But he's not a woman. And he's never going to be a woman. We're thankful for that, yes? Most men don't derive pleasure from feminine banter. It can wear them out … quicker than we realize. Men use fewer words, but more about that later …

Bottom line: There is a simpler way. Before you start talking, give him the bottom line. Is there a problem you need his help with? Or is the current problem that you just need someone to tell a story to?

If you let him know that you just want to share something with him – pleasant or unpleasant – just because he's your Best Friend … that you just want him to listen and be interested in you … that you don't want him to fix any particular problem … that you'll only talk for five minutes, he'll most likely be happy to do that for you.

But only for five minutes – really.

Why do men get worn out by our long stories? Because they're working so hard to try to find the bottom line. And they look for the bottom line at the end of each sentence. But then we start a new sentence, and he still has the previous sentence in his head, and the new sentence doesn't seem to follow the previous sentence … and he glazes over. Poor guy.

Just remember that his problem-solving is another way he shows you that he cares for you. He doesn't want to see you anxious or hurting or distressed or angry ... especially angry at him. Which leads us to his next purpose ...

My Pleaser

This is one that so many women don't completely grasp. Most men I meet – even the ones who are coming to counseling to work through some very difficult relationship issues – simply want their wives to be happy. Their bottom line is that they desperately want to please their wives, but they just can't seem to figure out how to do it. Sadly, most men would be willing to settle for an end to the arguing.

Men hate conflict. Many shut down in an attempt to slow it down ...or to avoid it altogether. We call that *stonewalling*, and it invariably has exactly the opposite effect than the one he's hoping to achieve. (See Chapter 25.)

So men often give in to their wives just to bring an end to the argument. When he gives in to you, he gives up the Power he needs in order to be your Protector, Provider, and Problem-solver just for the sake of ending the argument. It's emasculating.

Although he should never just do whatever you say just to make you happy, he shouldn't tune you out either. Men in successful marriages are open to their wives' feedback. But when either person becomes a doormat, it creates different problems. You're a couple, dancing as one, remember? Both people matter.

Please believe him when he says he really wants to see you actively, joyously happy ... especially with him. When that happens, you both win, and you both get to participate in the Dance of Romance. You win because you're happy, and he wins because he got something right. You won't believe what this does for a guy ... to be able to see his woman smile. So let him know when he gets it right ... with a smile. But more about that in Chapter 22, "Home Improvement."

Immortal, Invisible, God Only Wise

Immortal, invisible, God only wise,
In light inaccessible, hid from our eyes,
Most blessed, most glorious, the Ancient of Days,
Almighty, victorious, Thy great name we praise.

Unresting, unhasting, and silent as light,
Nor wanting, nor wasting, Thou rulest in might;
Thy justice, like mountains, high soaring above
Thy clouds, which are fountains of goodness and love.

To all, life Thou givest, to both great and small;
In all life Thou livest, the true life of all;
We blossom and flourish as leaves on the tree,
And wither and perish—but naught changeth Thee.

Great Father of glory, pure Father of light,
Thine angels adore Thee, all veiling their sight;
All praise we would render; oh, help us to see
'Tis only the splendor of light hideth Thee.

~ Walter C. Smith, 1876

STAGES OF A MAN'S LIFE

Another way that men are different from women is in the course of their lifespan development. And where they are in the process of life will affect their Leadership capabilities, as well as the style of Dance they choose.

As those best suited to be Followers, women tend to be Adapters. That is, we can pretty much bloom wherever we're planted … if we *want* to bloom, that is. (Yes. Mixed metaphors again.) We adapt to men, and we adapt to children. We adapt to our family of origin, and we adapt to the society in which we live. Whether we want to admit it or not, the course of female development is often highly dependent upon what's going for others.

For example, it's not unusual for a woman to obtain a college degree, build a career, then marry and have children. When the kids come along, a woman may take a break from her career or cut back on her hours in favor of being a mom.

It's also not unusual for a woman to marry young, help her husband through college, and forego her own degree and career until her children are older or out of the house.

Nor is it unusual for a woman to forego marriage to take care of an aging or ill parent or other family member. She may also join the military, fight in war, or run a business. For women, the possibilities seem endless.

Men adapt, too. But in general, their development is a bit more predictable ... a bit more linear. And with all the challenges that brings, they have even more reason to need women ... and for women to be really great at adapting.

During my studies at Christian universities, several professors drove home the idea that truth is truth. And that all truth is God's truth. That is, who God is and how He reveals Himself in His Creation cannot be in conflict with one another. If anything is true, it's because God created it, and it belongs to Him. All of it.

My professors explained the differences between *special revelation* and *general revelation*. Special revelation is Truth that is given us through the Word of God, whereas general revelation is available to anyone who bothers to take the time to observe His Creation. In brief, you don't have to be a Believer to observe God's truth in His Creation. You don't even have to be a psychologist! Go figure.

Nevertheless, several psychologists have proposed models of male development, and you can read about some of them in my book, *Mothers and Sons: How the Maternal Attachment Experience Affects Boys' Emotional and Social Development.* I could share that same information with you here, or I could offer you other models to consider. I could even review several non-psychologist approaches. There are many of each from which to choose.

However, I'm opting for a more light-hearted approach here, using men that are in my own life as examples. So my own developmental model includes the following four stages: Superhero, Adventurer, Hero, and King.

And again, I must caution that the following information *probably* applies to most men. There are always exceptions, so it will be up to you to check this part out for yourself ... to see if any of it applies to *your* man.

The Superhero

My grandsons are the greatest. At this point, I have two, with one more on the way. Of course, they are all awesome men-in-the-making. But only one is old enough to be my superhero ... so far.

All men want to be a hero, which comes easily to them, as noted. By 4 years of age, my oldest grandson had already figured out how to be my *Super*hero!

Depending on what day it was, he'd be Spider Man, Batman, or Superman – and he'd save me from the "mean guys" who lurked in the corner of my family room then sneaked up the stairs and into my walk-in closet. These villains would have gone undetected, but My Little Superhero knew they were there. He slung his web to capture them, then proudly announced that he had saved me, and I didn't have to be afraid anymore.

I remember the first time he saw me heading to a Saturday night dance. He stood back with the most delightful grin on his face as I descended the stairs. Totally fascinated, he watched intently as my skirt skimmed the steps behind me. "Gramma Debi," he sighed. "You look just like a Princess."

The most important work of boyhood is what he does for play ... pretending ... practicing for life and imagining the man that he wants to become. In acting out his dreams of manhood, my grandson created the most delightful story of "The Princess and the Superhero," which we played daily. And The Princess was me! ... unless his mom was around, that is. Then he had to choose. We'd give him a hard time of it, of course, and he adored having two women fight over him. What a great kid!

From the time boys are big enough to walk and to talk until they reach puberty, they engage in the serious business of acting out their ideas of what it means to be a man. They imitate their fathers, as well as what they see on television. It's always amazing and dramatic and larger than life. And it's a total joy to behold.

And it's often risky ... not that they're necessarily aware that it's risky ... but because it's fun and because it brings them so much pleasure. Boys also need freedom to explore ... to see what happens when you drop a raw egg off the front porch ... or put your salamander in a kitchen sink full of milk. It even makes sense – from his perspective – that he prove his ability to put an entire frog in his mouth.

Dancing With a Superhero

And while he's busy being a Superhero, he needs a Princess ... a woman who can imagine with him and who will join in his Dance of Play. FYI: There's still a boy inside every man ... even inside your grandpa! So always be ready to play!

However, our tendency as mothers, grandmothers, aunts, sisters, teachers, and babysitters may be to squelch his boyish explorations ... to make him act safe and sane ... when he's neither one ... and isn't supposed to be.

And no, he's not supposed to be clean all the time either. Number One Son could actually *create* dust, and he loved to collect rocks ... which were usually covered with dirt, of course. And he also collected bottle caps, which were both dirty *and* sticky. Ah, "The Joy of Life!" (So reads his high school yearbook ad ...)

Number Two Son appeared to be such a neat little guy, so his dirt could sneak up on you. We had an out-of-town guest for dinner one evening, and his father commented that he needed to wash his face. In his sweet little 3-year-old voice he said, "Why? Do I got some doi-ty on me?" Then he methodically lifted a dirty sock from his lap and wiped his mouth with it!

Before Number Three Son could even walk, he had a refined skill for getting dirty ... sort of like the character Pigpen in

Charles Schultz's *Peanuts* cartoons. I'd always get everyone else ready, then dress him ... and he'd still manage to create a mess before we made it to the car.

We moved into a new house the summer he was three years old, and our new lawn was being seeded. (We lived in the Midwest, and most people didn't use sod in those days.) We had one section of the lawn where all the neighborhood boys would play with their toy trucks, and Number Three Son would get so covered with dirt that I'd have to turn the garden hose on him before I'd even let him in the house!

The Adventurer

Number Three Son married his college sweetheart, and their wedding programs contained pictures of them as children. What cute little blue-eyed blondes they both were! The photos that linger in my mind, however, were those taken when they were teenagers. My very pretty daughter-in-law sitting on a horse, complete with English riding gear. A very classy girl. And my son straddling his own trusty steed ... a motorcycle, of course. What is it about a child on a motorcycle that makes a mom nervous?

Once puberty strikes, a boy begins to connect his Superhero-self to Real Life Adventure. At this point, he's all about enjoying new experiences and mostly ... well, just having fun. Risky behavior abounds ... at least from Mom's point of view. Baseball, basketball, football, diving, and driving.

Secret treks to Who Knows Where and Don't Tell Mom. And doing things that only a boy's logic could imagine.

Which reminds me of Number Two Son – accidentally locking a friend's keys in the trunk of his car in the middle of the night at Someplace You're Not Supposed to Be and calling home with a lame excuse about why he was going to be late ... then getting caught red-handed anyway.

... And Number One Son – getting his car stuck in the mud at church in the middle of the night because he didn't want to walk across the field to the basketball goal and risk ruining the Nikes he'd borrowed from his roommate ... so he drove instead. It seemed like a good idea at the time.

That's just the tip of the Adventure Iceberg. It wouldn't be fair to tell it all, lest their own children find out what they were really like as teenagers. So enough said. It's pretty obvious that boys don't think like moms do. And I have to wonder: Why do so many of these adventures happen in the middle of the night? It's a wonder any of them make it through to adulthood!

Dancing With an Adventurer

Dancing with an Adventurer requires an ability to be a bona fide Adventuress. If you're not into it, you'll miss out on some of the best fun a girl can have.

Guys who marry young will still be into adventure. It will pass ... at least in part. Some guys hang on to this stage as long as they can.

If this sounds like your man, you might want to read a book by John Eldredge – *Wild at Heart: Discovering the Secret of a Man's Soul*. Some men don't relate to his take on what it means to be a man, but it will give you another way of looking at the adventurer that – at some level – does exist in every man.

Although some guys aren't all that into the Great Outdoors, they will get excited about another brand of Adventure. It'll be up to you to watch for it.

The Hero

Heroes are everywhere. We just don't notice them. And therein lies the problem. Men love to be heroes, and they work very hard at it ... no matter how old they are. However, in terms of the stages of male development, a Hero is a man who has found his own Princess in Real Life and is in the process of building a career and family with her.

Unfortunately, this can be one of those Seasons that can create a Plethora of Problems for married couples. He's working hard to provide *for* his family, and she just wants him to spend time *with* his family. Both are very important, but they argue and arrive at Nowhere.

Dancing With a Hero

A Hero needs a partner, a Helpmate, for sure. So if you're dancing with a Hero, you'll need to get good at recognizing everything he's doing for you, even while you're assisting him in finding a balance between work, family, and play. The temptation is to nag ... to become his mom. Trust me, no guy wants to be married to his mom – no matter how wonderful he says she is!

If you're currently married to a Hero – and most of my counseling clients are – you may inadvertently be making matters worse – simply because you don't understand how his mind works. If he's building a career, it's probably deeply into One Track Mode. And if your Dance isn't going well, you'll want to pay particular attention to Chapter 21, "What a Man Needs," Chapter 22, "Home Improvement," and Chapter 26, "Sex Means More Than You Realize."

The King

 I used to think I could never fall in love with a middle-aged man. They all seemed so b-o-r-i-n-g ... and so o-l-d. (My sincere apologies to my middle-aged male friends.) And old guys seem to think they know everything ... so they always give you advice.

At this point, I've been pretty independent for a very long time. Plus, I'm still really young at heart, so I'd been thinking, "Give me a Hero who's still in the process ... and who still has a fair amount of the Superhero and the Adventurer in him. No, Sir-ee! No boring old guy for me!"

Boy, was I wrong! I've learned that men who've raised their families and established careers are Wonderful! They're truly Kings! A King knows who he is, so you don't have to worry about him trying to prove himself at your expense. Plus, he knows what he likes and doesn't like, and won't waste time on anything he doesn't find enjoyable.

Although a King may be unsure of himself when it comes to a woman (especially if he's dancing single), he's fully aware of what he has to offer.

And he'll give you advice – not because he thinks you're stupid or wrong or incapable – but because he wants *you* to benefit from his experience! How sweet is that?

Dancing With a King

When you appreciate who he is and what he has to offer, you'll find that a King has absolutely the very best balance of Superhero, Adventurer, and Hero within him! He needs a Partner who accepts him just as he is – a woman who knows, understands, and respects his needs and desires. We'll cover that in Chapter 21. But first, an important issue!

Chapter 20

RESPECT THE MAN CAVE

Even though I walk through the darkest valley,
I will fear no evil, for you are with me;
your rod and your staff, they comfort me.
~ Psalm 23:4

I love to listen to men because they always have something of value to say ... especially older men. Pop Quiz for you:

Your man doesn't tell you what he needs from you when he's struggling with something because:
    a) he's flooded (emotionally)
    b) he doesn't know what he needs from you
    c) all of the above

Correct answer: c) all of the above.

An understanding of men necessarily includes a healthy respect for the Man Cave. But as women we typically have a really hard time with it. We have nothing to compare it to, so it simply doesn't make sense to us.

But it makes a lot of sense to men.

When we're worried about something, we usually want someone to walk and to talk though it with us. For the most part, our American culture has trained us to do just that.

However, that same culture taught him to do the opposite! Remember the story of what happens to the toddler boy on the playground? His early experiences were the beginning of his education in The Boy Code. He learned that a man has to appear tough – a Sturdy Oak – in order to be loved and respected. And he learned that a man must figure out his own problems and deal with any vulnerable emotions – anger, sadness, fear, hurt, grief, shame, guilt, and doubt – on his own.

So that's what he does, and he does it in the Man Cave.

Looking at it from our side of the wall, the Man Cave feels like stonewalling at best and abandonment at worst. But the Man Cave isn't stonewalling at all … unless a women tries to break though. Then he has Double Trouble on his hands.

Simply knowing that her man is struggling is not enough, because that only serves to trigger a woman's natural desire to reach out and encourage him … to get him to talk to her … to try to convince him that she is his Safe Haven.

But a lifetime of experience has taught him otherwise. Her efforts to connect will feel like an invasion to him … and/or add to his sense of guilt and shame that he hasn't got a solution. Both of which will result in an immediate increase in his defensiveness – usually by strengthening his wall.

And being shut out makes her more anxious … worried about him … and about herself. It feels like the Beginning of the End to her, and she often doesn't understand why. So she tries to fix it. But first she has to get through the wall. Drastic times call for drastic measures … so she hauls out the Wrecking Ball. I mean, after all, doesn't the Bible say it's not good for the man to be alone?

You can see where this is going, right? Nowhere.

Absolutely Nowhere.

"So what do I do? I suppose you expect me to sit down on the curb outside the Man Cave and just wait for him to come out?" you ask in your frustration. "If I do that," you reason, "he'll never come out!"

Nope. There's so much more you can do to help him! Yes, you're right about it not being good for him to be alone. But how you choose to partner with him in times like these will make all the difference in the world for you both!

First, let him know you notice that something's up with him. And keep your remarks simple. You might say, "I feel like you're disappearing, and suspect that something's troubling you. Life is so hard on men. I don't know how you do it."

Second, shut up. Yes, I know I shouldn't tell you to "shut up" because my grandson told me those are "bad words." But it's *essential* that we learn this Important Fact:

> *When it comes to his emotions, something said in fewer words holds more meaning for a man.*

He listens in sentences, remember? So don't worry if he doesn't respond or offer more. Your empathy did register with him. And it made a difference. It made an immediate, significant difference. And by not probing him with a lot of questions or pounding him with further verbiage, you're demonstrating your respect for the Man Cave.

Third, if he does share his struggle, your job is simply to listen. He's testing the water to see if you're safe. You are. Your goal is to learn about him. No advice. No suggestions. Let your words be few and empathic (e.g., "sounds hard"). And, most importantly … keep what he does share between you and the Lord.

Which brings us to the fourth and most important thing you can do. Pray for him. He doesn't necessarily need to know that you're praying, though some men do feel supported by that fact. If you do tell him, say it once a day at most.

Most Christian women pray for their men, of course. But what is the content of your prayers? Are you just telling the Lord to help him to get his act together so your life will be easier, or are you sincerely interested in meeting his needs?

If you want to pray effectively for your man, you'll need to get into the cave with him ... spiritually and emotionally speaking, that is, rather than verbally or invasively as noted. Don't insist he talk about his feelings because he may not understand them himself.

Because you're not a man, you'll need a spirit of wisdom and revelation (Ephesians 1:17) that will enable you to pray for him in accordance with God's will and perspective on the situation. Yes, you may have some great ideas, but this may not be the best time to share them with your man. Wait upon the Lord, trusting that He cares a lot more about what's going on with your man than you do.

A final word: Keep the content of your prayers between you and the Lord. Your husband's vulnerability is not a subject you should be sharing with your mother, your sister, or your girlfriends.

And that's the Truth about what he needs from you while he's in the Man Cave.

More on his needs in the next chapter ...

Chapter 21

WHAT A MAN NEEDS

The Lord God said, "It is not good for the man to be alone.
I will make a helper suitable for him."
~ Genesis 2:18

Oftentimes, a man in couples counseling will want to focus
only on what will make his wife happy. That's very noble,
and I love that about men. In fact, I've come to believe that
every man's primary goal is to make his woman happy. And
as I'm thinking about this now, I must confess that every
man I've ever talked to about women has confirmed this as
one of his Primary Life Goals: to make his woman happy.

So after a few counseling sessions, I ask the man how things
went the previous week. He usually says, "It was better."

When I ask what was different – what made it better, his
response is simple: "We didn't argue."

For him, that's progress. And it is for her, too.

But there's a lot more to it than that.

I remember one man in particular, a former Marine. We'd
been talking for several weeks about various ways his wife
wanted him to meet her emotional and relational needs.

When I asked him what he needed from his wife, he smiled. "Nothing. I just want her to be happy."

Essay Question vs. Multiple Choice

This guy wasn't telling the whole story. But it's been my experience that men just aren't good at answering those essay-type questions. "What do you need from your wife?" feels like a blank page to him. And because he was raised to deny his own needs, he has a hard time recalling them.

However, men are great at recognizing the "right answer" when they hear it ... kind of like a multiple-choice test. As a former student and professor, I know those kinds of exams are easier on students and professors alike in that both enjoy less work than with the essay questions. The student merely needs to select the right answer ... it's right there in front of him. And the prof simply runs the Scantron through the machine, which makes grading a cinch.

So did I help the Marine out by giving him a multiple-choice question? No, not exactly. I affirmed what he'd just told me about his desire to make his wife happy, and how much it means to him to be able to be with her without the arguing.

Then I turned to his wife, restating what he'd said about not needing anything from her. She nodded and confirmed that he won't tell her what he needs either.

With a sense of hopelessness and confusion, she reported, "I ask him that all the time, and he always says, 'Nothing'."

I validated her experience and told her that the vast majority of men won't say what they need – and they do so for a variety of very good reasons. I told her what I've learned about men's needs. The Marine nodded – as most men do – as I provided a list of his needs for his wife. Then I gave him a chance to reply. "Yeah, that's it! That's exactly what I need." She gets it, and now both of them are happy. Ta da!

The Most Important Factor

The first thing a man needs from his wife is evidence of her own confidence. So many times when things go wrong, we start trying to change ourselves. He picked you because he likes who you are.

Here's an example: Cathy grew up dreaming of the perfect world. Pretty dresses. An elegant, well-situated Castle. And, of course, a Handsome Prince.

While they were dating, Mark fit the handsome-prince role perfectly. He was charming and thoughtful, and loved surprising Cathy with little gifts. And, of course, Christmas was the best! Everything he put under the tree for her was perfect – almost as though he'd kept detailed notes about all the things she had talked about throughout the year.

He certainly wasn't like her father, who never seemed to be around when she needed him. There was no doubt that her dad had always been a great Provider, working his way to the top of his company, but it had occupied most of his time and seemingly all of his energy.

For as long as Cathy could remember, her mother had complained that she felt like she'd been a single parent from the beginning. Yet for some reason, her mother seemed to blame herself for Dad's lack of involvement with the family. She was always upbeat, cajoling, trying to entice him to do things with the family. But it rarely worked.

Cathy felt it, too. It was as though she wasn't important to her dad. When she was a little girl, she tried her best to be cute and funny to get his attention. Sometimes it worked. Sometimes it didn't. She could never figure out why.

But Mark was so very different! At last Cathy had the male attention she had craved. Mark said – and demonstrated through his behavior – that his world revolved around her.

Reflecting on their first night in their new home after the honeymoon, Cathy remembered how shocked she was by Mark's sudden lack of responsiveness. All she had asked was that he turn off the TV so they could go to sleep. He'd acted as though he didn't even hear her!

So she turned on the charm. Nothing.

She became more vocal. Still no response.

Moving to the living room was her most dramatic ploy. She thought that would surely let him know she was upset and that he would follow her. But he didn't.

She had no idea what to do. Her sugar-and-spice routine had failed, and she couldn't figure out why. So she pulled away ... retreated, hoping Mark would feel guilty enough to follow her. He was such a wonderful man.

She *must* be doing something wrong. But what was it?

All these years later she still wonders what went wrong. She tried hard to make everything nice, but she failed miserably. And Mark felt like he had failed as well, though he never said as much. He only withdrew more and more as the years went by. Both of them got lost somehow.

Had Cathy known what was going on in Mark's mind, she might have approached the whole situation differently. And it would not have required emotional contortions and resorting to guilt and manipulation to get her needs met ... or his. In fact, Mark and Cathy might have both come out ahead of the game that night – a little more skilled in the Dance of Romance.

Another example comes from a question asked repeatedly by unmarried women. "We were getting along so well! I don't understand what happened. Why did he disappear? Did I do something wrong?"

Many single men tend to move forward in a relationship, then seem to back up – which can be a frustrating twist on the Country Two-Step for the women they've expressed an interest in. Some women take it all in stride, whereas others begin to struggle with their self-confidence. And we know that women with low self-confidence can be very, very unattractive to men. Which can lead to that old, inevitable self-fulfilling prophecy about being unlovable.

So what's a woman to do? Some decide to "fake it 'til you make it." So do you pretend to be something you're not? Seriously. How can that be helpful?

Others say "dump the dude!" … But isn't that like quitting before you get fired? So do you pursue him? No, that never works. It's very unflattering to say the least.

Time for a reality check.

First of all, whenever a man appears to be taking a step back from a relationship, that may or may not be the reality. Remember that men don't think or behave like a woman, so there's absolutely no point in judging him according to the standards of the Ideal Woman. He may just be busy.

He may also be taking a relational time out … and thinking about where he needs to lead next. If he truly cares about you, he'll give your relationship a lot of thought and prayer. Being a Leader in the Dance of Romance is an awesome task that can feel overwhelming. A good man will want to get it right. So he may need to spend some time in the Man Cave.

And it may not be something you need to figure out right now. Let the Lord do that for you. In a word, pray.

Although it's true that a woman's self-esteem relies heavily on what she thinks her man thinks of her, it shouldn't rule her life. Your self-esteem and your self-confidence must be based on the unconditional love of Christ.

If you're a Christian, reconnect with Jesus daily ... if not moment-by-moment (1 Thessalonians 5:17). And if you've not yet accepted Him as your Savior, you are invited to do so right now. He's right there with you ... wherever you are in the process of life ... eagerly waiting to hear from you!

Having Jesus in your heart makes all the difference in the world! You can place your full confidence in Him. As you grasp the reality of God's love for you, you'll realize you can fully trust Him to take care of and guide you. And if the guy really is going away, it's probably for your best.

Needy or Openly Vulnerable?

The second thing a man needs from a woman is her honesty about who she is in terms of her own vulnerability. In other words, a Real Man needs a Real Woman to dance with.

Neediness gets such a bum rap. As one of my mentors told me, "To say that someone is too needy is like saying they are too human." And he was right. We are all *very* needy. We absolutely cannot survive very long without one another ... or a facsimile thereof. Do you remember "Wilson," Tom Hanks's volleyball friend in the movie *Castaway*? Human contact is so essential that we will create a face into which we can gaze. Animal, vegetable, or mineral, we derive great comfort in believing that we are not alone.

So if nothing is wrong with being needy, why are so many men so turned off by it? My guess is that it has nothing to do with any lack of empathy. Most men are *wonderfully* empathic. However, inexplicable emotion quickly becomes difficult for most of them because they can't figure out what the problem is – what it is that you need, what they can do to help. He might wish he could say, "Help me help you."

So let's go with vulnerability. By all means, do tell him how you feel. Just be brief and specific. It's also okay to cry ... as long as you give him something to do that will help you feel better. This is one of those times when he's guaranteed to win ... if only you'll help him figure out how.

A word of caution is needed here. Be sure you're honestly sharing your needs, concerns, or feelings, and not that you're getting into manipulation or guilt or attempting to fix whatever you think is wrong with him. We'll talk about how to help him become a better man in Chapter 24. But for now … let's keep working on you …

Have a Life of Your Own

Guys love to give to us, but interestingly enough, they're most inclined to be there for us when we don't appear to need them. That's a confusing comment, even to me, and I'm the one who just wrote it! But it's true. If you're passionate about your life, he'll naturally work harder to find ways to contribute to your life. He'll want to be a part of your life because you make his brain fire in the most delightful of ways. He won't say that, of course. But you'll know it because of how much likes to be around you.

No, this is not manipulation. We really *do* need to get a life of our own … something that God has called us to do … our unique contribution to His Kingdom. You'll feel the energy, and so will he! It will draw him to you just like a moth to a flame. In fact, your passion will inspire *many* men to want to help – the kid bagging your groceries, your dentist, and even your grandpa. And there's a bonus if he happens to be a love interest (e.g., husband, possible husband) in that he'll also see your passion for life as Totally Hot! ;)

Do You Wanna Dance With *Me*?

I've heard it said that there's a reason why bridegrooms are all dressed alike … Because it doesn't really matter what man you plug in to the role. It's only the bride that counts. The man just isn't that important.

You may chuckle about that, but it feels true to many men.

A woman is frequently surprised if she hears that her man feels like he's simply not that important to her … that he doesn't believe he's very high on her list of priorities.

In fact, he might feel like he's not even *on* her list! He may believe that he's nothing more than a paycheck to her ... something to be used up by her. And he doesn't want sex in exchange for his paycheck. He honestly wants to feel emotionally *connected* to her, but he just can't figure out how to make it happen.

Yes, he knows you want to dance, but he may be having a really hard time believing that it's *him* you want to be dancing with!

There are so many ways men try to connect with us ... to ask us to dance with them.

And it requires a tremendous amount of courage to ask ... especially if they have been shot down a lot.

However, each time a man gets a "yes," he's encouraged to ask again ... and again ... and again ...

Here are just a few essential ways that you can say "yes" to the men in your life ...

#1. Your Attention

Men are only interested in *one* thing? Well, it's not sex.

Yes, it's true that sex with his wife is *one thing* that makes a man feel loved. But, what he wants most is your attention.

In fact, he's always needed a woman's attention.

Like most boys, all three of my sons were involved in sports. Swimming, soccer, baseball, basketball, football, and cross country. And one of the most important predictors of their enjoyment was whether or not mom was there to watch.

For example, as a little guy in his first swimming lessons, Number One Son stood there on the diving board shouting, "Mom! Mom!" to be sure I was watching before he'd jump. And just as soon as his little head bobbed out of the pool, he'd look in my direction and wait for his well-deserved cheer. Then back to the diving board for another plunge ... and more smiles from Mom!

Men don't change much in this regard. They crave female attention. Your attention will be especially important if he's a love interest (e.g., husband or possible husband).

Look at him adoringly when he talks to you. Listen intently to what he has to say. Why? Because every time he speaks, he's sharing something about who he is – his thoughts, his beliefs, his hopes, his fears, his values. Men share far more than we realize, but they do it differently than we do. And if he believes you're interested, he'll keep talking.

On the other hand, if you interrupt, interject, or make it about you, he'll assume you're just not into what he's saying and will stop talking. We do this far more often than we realize we do because of our female communication style. What to do then?

Be a safe person for him. Don't evaluate what he says or compare him to yourself or to another man. Don't probe or ask questions, unless you're simply saying, "Tell me more." And don't share intimate details with your girlfriends.

#2. Your Acceptance

My Superhero grandson was only three when he moved to California – with his parents, of course. And he loved going for leisurely walks around the neighborhood with me. Always drawn to flowers, he had to stop and smell each one along the way. I instructed him that we mustn't pick them because they belonged to my neighbors. So he'd patiently remind me as he admired their bright colors and imagined fragrance, "We can't pick your neighbor's flowers."

However, he didn't apply the same rule to flowers blooming in front of the bank or in the park or next to Carl's Jr. He'd race over and pick one as soon as he saw them, then present it to me with a gigantic smile on his sweet little face.

"Here! This is for you, Gramma!" he'd announce with great pleasure, fully expecting my reflected joy for the gift he so proudly bestowed. Of course, I was always very delighted … and I refrained from shaming him for picking the flower.

Men don't change in this regard either. Remember they still love to make us smile. No matter his age, whenever he sees you smile, it brightens his day … and his life!

You don't have to pretend that he's perfect, or that his gifts are perfect. When you accept what he brings to your life, you are accepting him. And that's a very good thing.

So the best response is very simple: Say "thank you" with a smile on your face. You'll make his day.

Have you ever responded to your guy's gift with some sort of critique? He "wasted" money on flowers. You'd rather have such-and-such. Why didn't he _____ (*fill in the blank*)? If you do that to him again and again, he'll be inclined to question the possibility of making you happy. And at some point, he won't even try anymore.

Remember that your man wants to be your hero – always. God designed him with a natural desire to protect you, to guide you, and to hold you – to make you happy – if you'll only let him. He won't do it perfectly. So you will need to let go of your tendency to correct him, to teach him, to give him advice – even about how to dance. Those messages tell him he's not good enough – that he will never be good enough – and that he'll never be able to make you happy.

#3. Your Affection

Several years ago, I read about an experiment that was conducted somewhere in the restaurant business. These researchers were exploring the value of touch in human interactions. Servers in the control group went about their work as usual, whereas servers in the experimental group were instructed to briefly touch their customer's hand while in the process of serving the food. The independent variable was *touch*, and the dependent variable was *the amount of the tip* the customer left for the server.

Guess what? Those servers who touched their customer's hand received much higher tips!

Seriously. Like we didn't see that coming?

We are all so hungry for human touch, and we rarely get that need met. Women, of course, have a better shot at it because it's more socially acceptable for them to hug one another. But we do more than just hug. We actually hold one another.

> **Q:** Do you know the difference between *hugging* someone and *holding* them?
>
> **A:** About 10 seconds.

But after a certain age, men are rarely held … unless they're having sex. Perhaps that's what makes sex so essential for a man's sense of well-being?

In fact, a number of forty-something husbands have said, "She never touches me anymore."

That's so sad … especially when you realize that their wives want to be touched as well. I'm not talking about sexual touch, and neither are these men. They're talking about day-to-day, nonsexual, incidental touch … an amazingly powerful connection with your partner.

So when dinner's ready tonight, don't holler at him to come and eat. Go to wherever he is and stand beside him, place your hand on his shoulder or arm, then smile and softly say, "Dinner's ready."

Then turn and walk away quietly. Even if he doesn't move a muscle or say a word ... or even come and eat ... you can be sure your touch and soft voice registered in his brain.

There's nothing more calming than making contact with the person you love most. So make physical contact as often as you can. You don't have to be dramatic about it. Start slow. Remember, his brain will notice even if he doesn't.

And if he's in the mood for sex, take it as a positive indicator ... that he needs to be held ... by you.

> **Hot Tip for Wives:**
>
> Kiss your husband
> ... passionately
> ... at least three times
> ... each and every day.
>
> He needs it!

#4. Your Appreciation

A simple "Thank You" goes a long, long way.

Enough said?
Yes, I believe it is.

#5. Your Admiration

This need is way more important than you might believe. And it's something you probably don't think about giving to him nearly often enough. Men need a woman's admiration. It's not an ego thing. It's an actual factual emotional need.

And this emotional need increases with his age! That is to say that a man in midlife needs to hear about his woman's admiration of him ... on a regular basis (i.e., daily). In fact, it's every bit as important as kissing him every day!

"Why is that?" you ask. Why should I have to tell him that I admire him? "Shouldn't he just be the man he's supposed to be without me having to pump him up all the time?"

A few years ago, I had the opportunity to work with a wonderful Christian couple who had gotten themselves into a big mess. They'd met in Bible college, graduated together, and married soon after. She raised five kids, and he worked his way up in his company from the ground floor to Vice President. She was there for the whole thing. She watched his successes ... and his failures. But she never thought to tell him how proud she was of all he'd accomplished. After all, he hadn't said much to her about what a great job she'd done raising their five kids. It just didn't seem necessary.

On the contrary, she'd become rather contrary. How's that for telling it like it was? In other words, she'd developed an edge to her – a critical spirit. Perhaps because she didn't feel like she held much value in today's world compared to him, she always seemed to have an angry tone to her voice. She didn't realize it, and he never said anything to her about it. She probably would have become more angry if he did.

Anyway, he just ignored his own need for her admiration. How could he ask for her positive feedback when it was so obvious that she wasn't happy with him or with much of anything he had been doing of late? Even about his being a wonderful grandpa for their new grandkids. He blocked the pain of her comments from his heart and mind, and went on with his work.

But someone did notice him. It seemed innocent enough. Just a compliment here and there. Nothing to alarm him ... or the woman who was so generous with her praise. But it wasn't long before he found himself looking forward to seeing her. One day he took her to lunch ... just to thank her for all the help she'd provided for his recent project. That was okay, wasn't it?

They say that if you put a frog in a pot full of hot water, he'll jump out immediately. However, if you put that same frog in a pot full of cold water and slowly turn up the heat, he'll sit in the pot until he cooks himself to death.

That's the truth about how many midlife affairs begin. A man has an unmet emotional need, and he doesn't think to ask his wife to meet that need. For a couple of reasons.

First, remember the Boy Code? Men never outgrow those instructions to never let anyone know you feel like a failure – or that you feel vulnerable. In other words, don't ask for your needs to be met. Deny them at all costs.

Second, a man usually avoids asking for anything – except maybe sex once in a while – because he dreads his wife's reaction, which can range from disregard to humiliation to anger. In his mind, it can only be a no-win situation. So he usually says nothing … that is, if he's even aware that he has an emotional need of any kind.

So he sets himself up as a frog in a pot. That's something we can change, so I'm working really hard to help wives become aware of what their husbands need. And to help them make it safe for them to ask for their emotional – and sexual – needs to be met. Despite what women believe, most men who have affairs in midlife are not trying to recapture their youth with a younger, sexier woman.

Don't get me wrong here! A husband's affair is *NEVER* his wife's fault. If he chooses to go outside his marriage, he is solely responsible for own his actions!

However, a wife can make it a lot safer for her man to talk about what might be missing in his relationship with her. And she can start by talking with him about these five needs and how well she's doing at meeting them for him. Here they are again:
1. Attention
2. Acceptance
3. Affection
4. Appreciation
5. Admiration

Now it's time to learn the Truth about how to change a man. Really? Really.

Chapter 22

HOME IMPROVEMENT

And we all, who with unveiled faces contemplate the Lord's glory,
are being transformed into his image with ever-increasing glory,
which comes from the Lord, who is the Spirit.
                                                        ~ 2 Corinthians 3:18

You've probably heard the saying that when a man marries a woman he's hoping she'll never change, whereas a woman marries a man hoping that he will. It's actually more than a hope for her. He may actually be her Main Project.

But men are not projects. They are people.

I don't like to be the bearer of bad tidings, ladies, but God only created one perfect man thus far. And he's required nearly six decades to refine! On the Brightside, however, if the Lord is doing such a great job on this one, I believe He can do the same with your guy! Your man can be so much more, and you can actually help him become *Your* Fearless Leader in the Dance of Romance!

Simply put, it's a woman's job to love her man and pray for him. It's God's job to make him grow ... and according to His plan, not hers. Your man wants to be your Leader in the Dance of Romance ... to protect you and to guide you and to hold you ... to choreograph the Dance to maximize your pleasure in being with him.

But much of the time we're shooting ourselves in the foot by doing all the things that *don't work* to change him … instead of doing things that *do work* to change him … things that he actually *wants* you to do to shape his behavior! Go figure.

What Doesn't Work?

Before we can begin to learn what works, we must recognize what doesn't. So I often begin my women's workshops with this simple fill-in-the-blank statement:

> * The thing that troubles me most about men is
> _____.

Then we discuss all the various ways we've tried to change whatever it is we don't like about them. None of it has ever worked, of course, but don't we keep doing the same thing over and over again, expecting different results? Wait! Isn't that the textbook definition of "crazy?" Yes, I believe it is!

There are several strategies that women try repeatedly in their attempts to change a man. Here's a very brief list of some of the things we've all tried … at one time or another … and the reasons why they don't work.

Hints

In plain, simple language: "Guys don't do hints." Why not? Because they don't even recognize them! Hints are clouded with Girl Code, which they can't even being to comprehend. So why rely so heavily on hints when they never work?

We hint that we'd like to go out to eat … or to Hawaii. Our word choices can be so vague that men are often left in the dark about what it is we're saying … or that we were even saying anything of significance at all!

We say, "Notice anything new?" Which is as dangerous as, "Does this outfit make me look fat?" It feels like a setup to him … like a trap … especially if past conversations have resulted in your anger. Of course, we know that your anger comes from having your feelings hurt. So why not avoid that probability altogether ... by setting him up to win right from the start?

One poor husband was painfully unaware of what his wife needed and wanted or even what she liked! He wanted so badly to please her, but he kept tripping over himself in the process. We were talking about their sexual relationship in one very tearful session, and I asked his wife to share with him just one thing that she liked.

She refused and said with an angry tone, "No, I'm not going to tell him. I shouldn't have to tell him. He should just know. If I tell him, then he'll do it, but only because I told him to, not because he wants to."

So her expectation was that he should read her mind? The last I knew, men and women dwell in very different bodies with very different designs. What's pleasurable to one is not necessarily the most enjoyable for the other. How can he possibly know unless she tells him? ... And just exactly what's wrong with him doing something that he knows would bring her pleasure?

Having said that, I really do understand her struggle. Most women are at least a little ambivalent about their sexuality. However, life is so much easier when we're direct. I know we weren't brought up that way, but sometimes we need to acquire new skills ... and new confidence ... in ourselves and in our partner.

Criticism

Women respond to criticism. It changes us. For example, I was wearing my favorite periwinkle blue blouse one day, and another woman told me that I really don't look good in that color. Now I happen to know for a fact that periwinkle blue is actually one of my very *best* colors. It makes my eyes appear more blue than they already are ... and they are already pretty darn blue. No, I've not stopped wearing that blouse. But I do make note of what I'm planning to wear on the days I know I'll be seeing her.

"How crazy is that?" you ask.

Pretty darn. But it's what we women do.

Men don't operate that way. Criticism only serves to rally their defensiveness, so it has the opposite effect on them. They'll go ahead and do it anyway ... or avoid the person ... or hide what they're doing.

One thing is sure: Criticizing a man will backfire every time.

Comparison

Many of us – but certainly not all – care way too much about what others are thinking of us ... probably because we're constantly judging one another.

Our standard: our concept of the Ideal Woman. Of course, none of us can measure up to that! And then we expect a *man* to measure up to the Ideal Woman?

"How crazy is that?" I ask.

Pretty darn. But it's what we women do.

Comparing our man to the Ideal Woman ... or to *anyone* ... is crazy. He's unique, and God loves him right now ... right where he is ... exactly the way he is. And if Our Holy God loves him, how can we dare to think we have a better idea? Honestly. We have neither the wisdom nor the power to change ourselves for the better, much less improve on a man ... for whom we have no blueprint in the first place.

Nagging

It makes him feel like a little boy. Which makes you feel like his mom. Not helpful for either of you. Enough said.

There is a better way, but first …

A Word (or Two) About Manipulation, Drama, and Guilt

A woman's good opinion should never be bestowed lightly or insincerely. When you pay him a compliment, it should be a totally honest one. Flattery is cheap and manipulative. Any woman who wants to improve her relationship must avoid manipulation and drama at all costs. Walk away from them both. Drama will drain him … and you, eventually.

Guilt trips are our specialty. We learn them from our moms. If you're not sure what one looks like, watch any episode of "Everybody Loves Raymond." Marie Barone is the Queen! Very funny on TV. Not so much in real life.

So what's the best way to improve your chances of getting your needs met? Ask for what you want … be specific and concrete … and accept his response whether it's *yes* or *no*.

Many women seem to be unaware of which behaviors might come across to others as manipulation, drama, or guilt. So ask your best friend – or a trusted counselor – to help you become aware of the times and situations in which you are most likely to engage in any of these tactics. Then cut it out.

What Does Work?

Clearly, a lot of our strategies don't work.

"So does anything work to change a man?" you ask.

Yes, and I'm so excited that I finally figured it out, and I can hardly wait to share it with you! Here's what I've learned … and how I introduce it to the women who come to my office for help with Home Improvement (also known as *Husband* Improvement).

At some point in couples counseling, I will say to the man, "Don't listen to this part."

Then I turn to his lady and let her in on His Best Kept Secret, "Men are like small children and dogs. If they are beaten or shamed for bad behavior, it just makes them avoid us. They may even cower when we come near.

"On the other hand, if we focus on what they do *right* and reward them for it, they'll go out of their way to get that reward again and again and again."

By this time, the man – although he's not listening – begins to smile and nod enthusiastically. "Ya!!! Do that!!!"

It's predictable. I have yet to hear a man say he's offended by my suggestion that his wife should treat him like a dog. And no wonder! Most women are kinder to their pets than they are to the man they love. How odd is that?

Think about it. You're happy to see your dog at the end of a long day, and you make sure Rover knows it. You talk to him sweetly and scratch him behind his ear. You take time to pet him and make sure he's fed. You even take him for a walk. And when he's a "Good Boy," you reward him with even more attention!

So there's really only one way to change a man: Positive Reinforcement

The real, scientific definition of *reinforcement* is anything that *increases* the likelihood that a *target behavior* will occur again.

In our case, the *target behavior* is anything that he does that makes us feel loved, cared for, and respected.

And reinforcement can be *positive* or *negative*. So at least in theory, both types of reinforcement increase the likelihood that the target behavior will occur again.

Negative reinforcement means that something unpleasant is taken away. For example, whenever you take an aspirin (*target behavior*) to deal with a headache, your headache will go away (*negative reinforcement*). Therefore, the next time a headache hits, it's more likely that you'll take an aspirin again ... because doing so the last time resulted in negative reinforcement. Or your man finally takes out the trash (*target behavior*), and your constant nagging goes away (*negative reinforcement*). So – at least in theory – the next time you start nagging, it's more likely he'll take out the trash because the last time resulted in negative reinforcement. But, that last example backfires sometimes, doesn't it? He may just learn to tune you out, which also ends the nagging ... and your relationship as you would like it to be.

I don't know about you, but headaches and nagging are not what I would want *my* man to have fresh on his mind whenever he thinks of me!

Reinforcement can also be positive in that something can be added, such as your "thank you" or your smile. He does something nice. You smile and say, "Thank you." Through positive reinforcement, you just increased the likelihood that he'll do something nice again.

So he does something nice yet again. So you smile and say, "Thank you." Now we've really got something good going!

In reality, that's the way it was in the beginning of your relationship. But most of us stop saying "Thank you" and begin to expect – rather than hope for and appreciate – good things from our guys.

Yes, it really is that easy to change a man ... for the better. But it took me years – and the advice of one great guy – to be able to put two and two together. I am a blonde, after all.

If I'd only paid attention sooner I could have figured it out way back when I was completing all those undergraduate studies. And I could have skipped grad school altogether ...

I missed the obvious when I was in charge of the Rat Lab in the Undergraduate Psychology Department at MidAmerica Nazarene University. During my senior year, I had the privilege to work with Dr. Arvin Oke on an experiment that won a Psi Chi Regional Research Award, and attended the Southwest Psychological Association Convention that spring in Houston, Texas, with a poster presentation of our work. Its title was "Selective Attention Dysfunction in Rats Treated With 6-Hydroxy Dopamine." Don't ask.

The first step in the experiment was to teach my baby rats to perform in a maze using a process called *shaping*. By rewarding them for *successive approximations* of the target behavior (their treat was just a tiny bit farther away each time), before long, these amazing little creatures had learned to sprint down the maze, select the correct sign, then open the door to collect their prize. A complex task for sure!

I didn't give my baby rats hints, nor did I criticize, compare, nag, or resort to manipulation, drama, and guilt when they made mistakes. None of that would have worked.

I was just very consistent in dispensing their rewards. After awhile, they performed the target behavior without a treat. But the treat made them so happy that I always gave it to them anyway. Why not?

Hmm. I wonder what men think of the Rat Lab example.
I don't think I want to know!

All that matters is … that it is, indeed, possible to change a man. And he'll love you all the more for doing it. After all, his goal is to make you happy, remember? You just need to let him know when he's succeeded!

 *Chapter 23*

LEARNING TO LEAD

*But the Lord God called to the man,
"Where are you?"*
~ Genesis 3:9

You remember Adam and Eve from The Big Inning? As the First Couple, they had it made, and they got in Big Trouble. Yes, we remember Eve started the whole thing. Deceived by the serpent, she ate the forbidden fruit first. Then convinced her husband to eat as well.

But she wasn't who God came looking for, was she?

Like it or not, the buck still stops here … with you, man. I'm constantly amazed by the weight of responsibility you guys carry on a day-to-day basis. Most of you do it with amazing style and grace. But it's truly a struggle. And I understand that … more than you will ever realize. My goal is to help your wife understand that, too.

I often recommend that women watch the movies *Fireproof* and *Courageous* because if a picture's worth a thousand words, then a great movie is worth a million more.

One of my favorite movie scenes is in *Superman: The Movie*. Lois Lane (played by Margot Kidder) is holding on tight to a strap, the only thing that's keeping her from falling to her death from the News helicopter that's hanging precariously off the side of the Daily Planet building in Metropolis. Her yellow hat drifts to the ground and lands right in front of Clark Kent (played by Christopher Reeve). He looks up and springs into action. Without a proper phone booth in sight – anyone remember those? – he spins around in the nearest revolving door and emerges as Superman.

Just as Lois's strength gives out and she begins her rapid descent, Superman swoops up to catch her. He tells her not to worry because he's got her.

Lois looks at him in amazement, then down at the ground, then back at her rescuer. With notable anxiety in her voice, she wonders who's got *him*!

Good question. All too often women expect men to be as invincible as Supermen, forgetting that they are human, too.

The words of the song "Lead Me" by Sanctus Real provide another – more true-to-life – expression of the pressure you men feel as our leaders ... and emphasize your desperate need for God's help to be the leader He wants you to be. If you haven't heard it, check it out on iTunes.

God First

Without a doubt, the First Thing you need to be the Leader you want to be is Jesus. He is absolutely The Essential One, not only for your well-being, but also for your family's well-being. If you're a Christian, reconnected with Him daily ... if not moment-by-moment (1 Thessalonians 5:17).

If you've not yet accepted Jesus as your Savior, you can do so now. He's there with you ... wherever you are in the process of life, and He's eagerly waiting to hear from you!

Take Advantage of Your Wife ... in a Good Way

Here are a few ways for you enjoy the benefits of Marriage ... receiving the love and moral support that you also need to be able to lead well ...

- Listen to her.
- Be her hero (i.e., treat her like a lady).
- Pay attention to her response to your leadership.
- Ask for what you need from her ... in addition to a great sex life, of course.
- Be courageous enough to allow yourself to be vulnerable with her.

If you're finding yourself stuck on any of these points, or if you think of anything else I can help you with, please do let me know. I look forward to hearing from you, whether you have a question, something to share, or encouragement to offer. I welcome it all!

> *My goal is to help men and women find better ways of relating to and enjoying one another, so I'm always looking for more opportunities to spread the Good News.*

I met a new couple at my church recently and was sharing about my specialty as a psychologist. I told them I teach classes for women about the psychology of men, and that we women often don't really get men. The guy immediately turned to his girlfriend and said, "I'll pay for you to go to her classes." He was totally serious.

At the end of each of my presentations, I encourage women to go home, sit down, and have a talk with their men. I tell them to share what they've heard from me and to ask their guys whether or not the information applies to them. The feedback I get is that men believe that I actually do get them. But I'm still a woman, so I know I don't get it right every time. Just ask the men who know me. Eh, guys?

The Bottom Line

Your woman is going to love the experience of following a godly man who knows how to lead gently and confidently. It's unforgettable joy!

Help us spread the word: Yes! There is Hope!

I believe that what we're doing in teaching men and women new, old-fashioned ways for them to engage in the beautiful Dance of Romance is important work, but I need your help. Send me your feedback. Send me your gal. And help us spread the Truth about Romance in the 21st Century!

Part 6
Life at the Tower of Babel

SPEAKING DIFFERENT LANGUAGES

Do you remember this story in Genesis 11?

> *Now the whole world had one language and a common speech. ... They said to each other, "... Come, let us build ourselves a city, with a tower that reaches to the heavens, so that we may make a name for ourselves ...."*
>
> *The Lord said, "... Come, let us go down and confuse their language so they will not understand each other."*
>
> *So the Lord scattered them from there over all the earth, and they stopped building the city. That is why it was called Babel – because there the Lord confused the language of the whole world.*

Okay, I'm just kidding. *Part 6* isn't really about *that* story. But many spouses have a hard time understanding the words that are coming out of the other person's mouth. Therefore, they feel like they're experiencing a sort of modern-day-marital Tower of Babel.

At the beginning of each counseling session, I check in to see how things have been going the previous week. A typical report: "We were sitting at Starbucks, having this great conversation, enjoying the morning. Then all of a sudden, she glazed over and refused to talk. I don't get it. I couldn't figure out what happened, and she refused to tell me."

Or I get a report like this: "I was talking about what we'd learning in our last session, and he suddenly got angry. He made a sarcastic comment, and then wouldn't talk anymore. I thought we were making progress. What happened?"

Like the folks at the Tower of Babel, everything seemed to be going well. Then all of a sudden, they lost their ability to communicate. They didn't realize it, but they were actually speaking different languages ... although it still sounded a lot like English to both of them. So let's explore why that happens so often between men and women.

Reuben and Rachel

Reuben, Reuben, I've been thinking
What a grand world this would be
If the men were all transported
Far beyond the Northern Sea!
Rachel, Rachel, I've been thinking,
What a good world this might be,
If we had some more young ladies
On this side the Northern Sea.

Reuben, Reuben, I've been thinking
Life would be so easy then;
What a lovely world this would be
If there were no tiresome men!
I'm a man without a victim,
Soon I think there's one will be,
If the men are not transported
Far beyond the Northern Sea.

Reuben, now do stop your teasing,
If you've any love for me;
I was only just a fooling,
As I thought of course you'd see.
Rachel, I will not transport you,
But will take you for a wife,
We will live on milk and honey,
Better or worse, we're in for life.

~ Harry Birch, 1871

Chapter 24

COMMUNICATION STYLES

To answer before listening –
that is folly and shame.
~ Proverbs 18:13

By now, we all know that a man is more sensitive than a woman. And he's vulnerable to different things than she is. So most of the time, a woman has absolutely no clue that she might be saying or doing anything that could be even remotely related to attack, blame, or criticism. This is where we need to understand the power of our language, and that words often hold very different meanings for a man than they do for a woman.

For example, I was counseling an engaged couple who had hit a roadblock on their way to the altar (metaphorically, not literally). As they struggled to understand one another, the woman looked at her fiancé and said, "I hate that I'm causing you so many problems. Maybe you'd be better off without me. Maybe it'd be better if I just walked away."

You can understand that statement, right? She sounds like she's willing to sacrifice her happiness for his.

That's not what he heard at all! What he actually heard was, "You'd better get your act together, Bud, or I'm outta here."

He was deeply wounded by her statement and didn't want it to show. So he stiffened his upper lip, and shut her out ... to protect himself.

When I told her how he heard her statement, she looked at us both in disbelief. Then he confirmed my translation from female expressive language into male receptive language. What she'd said was not what he had heard. His sensitivity to rejection ... to not being good enough ... to his failure to please her ... had colored the meaning of her words. He was listening though the filter of his emotions ... through his vulnerability and intense fear of being found inadequate.

I have learned to speak Two Languages.

As a woman, I get where gals are coming from. Sometimes, we can be amazingly direct in asking for what we want. At other times, we're not sure what we want. So we can also be pretty vague. Most of us have a hard time getting the men we love to understand us. It often feels like they're just trying to fix us. So, naturally, I speak "female."

As the mother of three sons, I've spent a lot of time studying the male experience. It's been a joy to watch my boys grow into men, marry, and become parents themselves. They've taught me a lot, and I'm still learning from them.

I've also studied the "Psychology Men and Traditional Masculinity" at the graduate and post-doctoral levels, and I've taught a university class on this very popular subject. What I've learned is that most women don't have a clue about men's experience, and that most men don't know how to explain it. So I've also learned to speak "male."

Differences in Body Language

Dr. Deborah Tannen is an expert in the field of interpersonal communication. She conducted a study of same-sex pairs of children (elementary school through high school) who were asked to take two chairs into a room and wait there for the researcher. I used to show video clips of this study in my class at Azusa Pacific University. It was amazing to watch. The female pairs were consistently engaged in face-to-face conversation as they were waiting for the experimenter. Conversely, the boys placed their chairs in a side-by-side configuration, rarely saying more than a few words to one another and avoiding eye contact.

So just how do you think this tendency might play out in conversations between men and women?

For a man, the face-to-face approach may make him feel like he's being challenged … especially if his woman is upset. Instinctively, he prepares to defend himself. And as every football fan knows, the best defense is a good offense. Which tends to be not-so-good for her.

Tip: One of the best ways to get a man – of any age – to talk to you is simply to engage in a joint activity that puts you side-by-side. Then let your conversation flow naturally, and before you know it, he'll be talking about more serious stuff.

Find an enjoyable activity (or semi-enjoyable activity, like washing dishes) that he would like you to do together that puts you side-by-side. Don't pressure him to start talking. Just listen and see what happens.

For women, the side-by-side approach may feel like her man isn't that interested in her … or that he simply doesn't give a rip about whatever she's saying. If she feels like she's being ignored, she'll "hit" harder with her words, trying to get him to respond to her.

Tip: If she appears to be upset about something, look into her eyes – with compassion. This isn't a stare-down, okay? Let her know you really want to understand her. Then give her a chance to speak. And listen carefully.

After a few moments, say, "Let me see if I've got this right. You're telling me that _____. Did I get it right? [Pause for her answer.] Did I miss anything? [Pause for her answer.] How can I help?" [Pause for her answer.]

If you get lost in what she said, just tell her you got lost. And ask her to try one more time. It's okay to tell her that you need her to give it to you bit-by-bit. She's read this book, too, right?

And … if you don't know what to say, then simply tell her, "I don't know what to say. I wish I did. I really wish I did." And if appropriate, make physical contact with her while you're talking. (See Chapter 13 for Tips about Touch.)

Differences in Quantity

As previously noted, men tend to listen in sentences. They're looking for a problem to solve or a purpose for relating the information. However, women tend to talk in paragraphs … sometimes volumes. Of course, sometimes a man talks more than his woman does. And sometimes a man is more anxious than his woman is. Yes, like anything else in life, there will always be individual differences. So keep that in mind … just in case you weren't already making allowances for your mate's uniqueness.

Differences in Word Choice

Here's another potential gender difference. Men tend to be more literal in their word choice, whereas, women tend to use general, more inclusive statements. It's how we were taught to be considerate and "relational" in our conversations. Remember Sean and Nicole? She wanted to stop and get something to eat, and Sean thought she was asking if *he* wanted something to eat. He took her question literally and said, "No." Her feelings were hurt.

Jim and Lisa had a similar misunderstanding. They'd made plans for a get-together at another couple's condo for a good home-cooked meal. At the last minute, her friend's husband contacted Jim to let them know they'd invited several others to join them for the evening.

As he shared the update with Lisa, she felt overwhelmed. She explained that she'd had a headache most of the day and was worried she might be coming down with a bug. But she hadn't wanted to back out on their plans because she knew the other wife would be going to a lot of trouble to fix a great meal for them.

However, now that it had become a group event, Lisa really wanted to stay home and rest. "I just don't feel like being around a whole bunch of people tonight," she explained. "How do you feel about rescheduling for another time?"

Jim's response was that he didn't want to cancel. Lisa was hurt and angry, and Jim couldn't figure out why. Can you?

He answered the question that she asked. He didn't want to reschedule. She asked how *he* felt about rescheduling. And he told her. But that wasn't her question. She was politely asking him if he would tell them she didn't feel well so they would need to reschedule.

But that wasn't what she said ... or what he heard. *Sigh.*

The Long and Short of It All

I fully realize I've only revealed a very small portion of the miscommunication iceberg here. Perhaps I'll need to write another book. Or maybe create a smartphone app that can translate Female into Male ...and *vice versa*. Or that gives you the perfect responses to anything the opposite sex says.

That'd be cool, eh?

Praps If You Address the Lady

P'raps if you address the lady
Most politely, most politely.
Flatter and impress the lady
Most politely, most politely.

Humbly beg and humbly sue,
She may deign to look on you,
But your doing you must do
Most politely, most politely, most politely!

Go you and inform the lady,
Most politely, most politely,
If she don't, we'll storm the lady
Most politely, most politely!

You'll remain as hostage here;
Should Hilarion disappear,
We will hang you, never fear,
Most politely, most politely, most politely!

~ Sir William S. Gilbert, 1884

THE ROLE OF EMOTIONS AND
UNDERSTANDING THE STONE WALL

Our emotions ebb and flow, especially when we're under stress. At one time or another in the counseling process, one or both partners will tell me that they are giving up on their relationship. And I always say I'll hang in there with them, even when they don't feel like going on. They usually keep going on because they love one another. And the more they trust in the Lord, the better things become for them both. Go figure.

Being created in the image of God, we experience a full range of emotions. Joy, anger, sadness, hurt, and fear are the basic ones ... with lots of variations. Unfortunately, due to the consequences of the Fall, guilt and shame are also very common in our human experience.

And God designed us in such a way that our emotions are primary. That is, feelings come first. He did it that way for some very good reasons. Mostly, He did it so that we could experience Joy in Him and in one another. So much for that lie about God not caring about our happiness, eh?

Our emotions are like a barometer designed to tell us that something is going on inside of us or in the space around us. So it's our job to figure out what our feelings are telling us about what's happening and what we can do in response.

No matter what anyone tries to tell you, your first response to any situation is emotional. You are created that way.

Information gets into your brain via two pathways. The emotional pathway is faster. Reason is the slower pathway. Emotions tell you action is needed ... now!

If you've ever seen a child run into the street in front of your car, you know what I mean. You slam on the brakes as soon as you see him. A few seconds later, your brain kicks in and tells you what happened. If you'd had to reason your way through the situation, your response would've been too late.

Emotion and Gender

Because women are emotionally sensitive and often express their feelings verbally and openly, many have assumed that women are more sensitive than men. Feelings are primary for a woman. However, they are primary for a man as well. It's just our *expression* of them that differs.

Volumes could be – and have been – written about the role of emotions, as well as gender differences in emotional experience and expression. It's a fascinating subject. But I want to give you some practical information, so I'll stick to a brief, mostly user-friendly example of how men and women use emotional information differently.

Analysis vs. Action

Stephania is watching TV, and she gets hungry. She begins to think about her recent food intake. She's torn between wanting the chocolate cake that's left over from Sunday's birthday party and realizing she probably already overshot her calorie-fat-carb-count for today with the extravagant lunch she had at Olive Garden with her best friend. She also calculates how much exercise she's had ... and how much exercise she can commit to over the next 24 to 48 hours. Her deliberation goes on for more than 30 minutes before she makes up her mind.

Eduardo is sitting beside her. He feels a slight hunger pang, gets up, goes to the fridge, and devours the chocolate cake. Stephania didn't stand a chance.

Generally speaking, emotions mean different things to men than they do to women. For men, emotions signal a need to take action. In short, fix the problem, or get away from it.

And if it's painful, don't go there, Dummy!

For a woman, however, feelings are there to increase your understanding ... especially in the context of relationship. (a) What does this mean? And (b) what should I do?

So much for men thinking they're the logical ones, eh?

Actually, men who tend to use a logical approach are also operating on the feelings-first basis. Because men are so sensitive to others, they may have a difficult time sitting with unresolved emotions ... whether those feelings are theirs or their mate's. Thus, "Let's get this problem solved!"

As previously stated, many women deal with anxiety and worry about almost everything ... most especially about their relationships. It's a driving force in their need to talk. Most women – not all – have difficulty "letting things go."

And so many men struggle with an enduring belief about their own inadequacy. Many a man carries an internal critic ... like an irritated coach who has taken up a permanent residence inside his own head ... one who's never satisfied with his performance and continually shouts out to him the play-by-play of what a failure he is. So whenever he hears his mate's anxiety – which usually sound a lot like anger – he adds the data to his backlog of failures.

And to protect himself, he builds a wall.

Understanding the Stone Wall

Fear is a primary emotion. It's meant to move us to action quickly because it protects us from harm. In our culture, we're mostly afraid of being vulnerable ... of being kicked while we're down. And our first reaction to fear is to hide.

But fear isn't the real problem!

The problem is hiding! We hide from God, which assures we won't receive His help, which we so desperately need. And we hide from one another.

That means we put up a "wall" to protect ourselves. Walls keep bad things out. But walls also keep good things out! Plus, our walls always hurt our partner.

What style wall do you build? Some prefer the walls of avoidance and withdrawal. Others build walls of criticism, attacking, or blaming to keep the focus off themselves. Both approaches are hurtful.

As a couples therapist, I've had a lot of opportunity to observe how hard women work at their relationships. When something's wrong, it's often the woman who notices it and wants to talk about it – to figure out what's wrong and fix the problem. Here's an example of a frequent complaint from our Relationship Survey:

> *We have problems agreeing on the way in which we will deal with problems. I want to deal with them when they come up, and he wants to think about it on his own for a long time and hope the problem goes away before we talk about it.*

Chances are, this woman won't be able to wait for him to bring up the problem again. She'll be miserable waiting on him to say something. At best, she'll feel like it's just not that important to him. At worst, she'll feel like SHE'S just not that important to him. As the hours and days tick by, she'll start to feel more and more anxious about their relationship.

So what is stonewalling?

Stonewalling is withdrawing or refusing to respond to your partner. For a man, it may be a response to his own confusion or due to his feeling overwhelmed. Remember that early in life, a man learns that he has to come up with the answers to problems on his own, so this behavior makes sense. However, the stone wall is a defensive move, which is different than the Man Cave discussed in Chapter 20.

For women, being stonewalled by her mate creates excessive anxiety – and anger.

Women Stonewall, too!

Now, for the surprising side of stonewalling: It's actually much more damaging to the relationship if the *woman* is the stone-waller!

Do you shut him out when he hurts your feelings or does something you don't approve of?

The female version of stonewalling can be subtle – refusing to talk to him for a few minutes – or dramatic – pouting, stomping out of the room, slamming doors, not speaking for days.

Ladies, observe your own behavior. Notice how often you stonewall in response to something he says or does. Remember, your stonewalling may be more subtle, so you'll have to be a diligent detective.

I received this comment from a visitor to our *Understanding Men* website. Notice how this man signed his comment. It reveals a ton about what he's experiencing!

Yours is the very first place I've visited that acknowledges the excessive damage caused by a female stonewaller.

Thank you. Thank you. Thank you.

I'm aware of my male ego. I can intellectualize this issue I'm faced with. I spend an inordinate amount of time qualifying the whys, the hows, and all the possible misinterpretations, before saying one word about how I'm feeling. But it doesn't matter.

At some point she will disengage. Here are her most popular ways:

- *I can't take this anymore.*
- *Can we talk about this later?*
- *Shouldn't you be working, instead of dealing with this? (This one really hurts.)*
- *Or she'll change the subject, and ignore what I'm saying.*
- *Or she'll pretend to listen, but meanwhile she's only in her own world.*
- *She'll play the victim "You're always complaining about me." My response is usually, "It's not a complaint, it's a concern, and if we managed to complete one of these conversations in a respectful and courteous way, we wouldn't be 'here' again."*

If I make one mistake (as she sees it) during attempt at communicating ... for example, raising my voice slightly ... she's done.

I eventually end up losing my temper, and saying something I feel I should apologize for saying (and always do so). She has a difficult time with apologies and acknowledging truth.

It's funny; I completely understand what she's doing. I was guilty of this in a previous relationship. However, this does nothing to heal the pain I feel.

*Here's the kicker ... other than this, she's the sweetest,
funniest, nicest person I've ever been with.*

*But my real need for what I term as "real intimacy,"
would seem to transcend this.*

Any thoughts would be deeply appreciated.

*Signed,
Emasculated*

My Response: Most people stonewall as a defense against
overwhelming anxiety. Think of it as her best attempt to
calm everything ... and everyone ... in the midst of what
feels like an impossible situation.

> *p.s. I almost forgot. What's your reasons for saying,
> "It's actually much more damaging to the
> relationship if the woman is the stonewaller"?*

My Second Response: According to research, men are more
emotionally and relationally sensitive. And they are less
likely to have the skills needed to repair the damage. That
is, it can be very, very difficult for a man to express his
vulnerability and to elicit the empathy and support he needs
from his partner.

Dealing With Conflict: Resolving Disagreements

How disagreements are resolved has a significant impact on
the level of satisfaction for both partners in a marriage, as
measured by a variety of relationship assessments, such as
the *Locke-Wallace Marital Adjustment Inventory*. The scoring
for this questionnaire weighs each answer differently
(higher is better) in response to the following statement:

> *When disagreements arise, they usually result in:*
> *(a) the husband giving in (0 points)*
> *(b) the wife giving in (2 points)*
> *(c) agreement by mutual give-and-take (10 points)*

Perhaps this is where men's greater emotional sensitivity comes into play? Or are we back to the fact that they need us ... and they need us a lot? Grantley Morris reported:

In a survey, marrieds were asked to name their best friend. Women typically named another woman, whereas most men either named their wives or confessed to there being no one in their entire world that they could call their best friend. This highlights how isolated most men are, and how dependent they are upon their wives for companionship. There simply seems to be something about being male that causes this aloneness. It is so basic that it is even found in the animal kingdom. In a wide range of animal species, females generally group together with each other and with the young, whereas mature males are loners, usually relating to their own species only to fight other males or mate with females.

It might take a husband years to realize just how mistaken was his presumption – and his wife's presumption – that his wife understood him. The typical husband's reliance upon his wife for companionship and emotional support makes it a chilling experience when he finally concedes she seems incapable of understanding him. Can you imagine how devastating it is to feel there is no one on the planet who knows and understands you to the degree that you crave and deserve?

If genuine, and not a mere pick-up line, "My wife doesn't understand me," are among the loneliest words in the English language. Not only that, the inability of most men to get close to each other usually leaves him feeling unable to turn to anyone for solace, unless it be another woman. He is strongly pressured either to try that, or try to protect himself from further hurt and disappointment by withdrawing somewhat from his wife and hope he can bury his pain in his job or other activities. When this happens, wives start complaining; never dreaming of the role they have played in making their husbands act this way.

Clearly, we need to learn how to be better at understanding one another ... and at recognizing the impact of our words!

When a woman attacks, criticizes, blame, or complains –
even if she isn't doing it intentionally – her man will feel like
a loser ... or he'll have to fight to avoid feeling like a loser ...
or he'll withdraw to avoid feeling like a loser ... all of which
will leave him feeling ... like a loser.

There's no way he can win at this game.

And, by the way, she can't win this way either.

The Bottom Line on Emotions

Men and women both experience a full range of vulnerable
emotions. But they express those emotions differently. Men
tend to take action, whereas women tend to want to talk
about how they feel.

However, both men and women are inclined to build walls
of self-protection – to keep themselves from being kicked
when they're down.

And the particular kinds of walls we choose to build are
painful for our partners.

Stay, Fredric, Stay!

Ah, leave me not to pine
Alone and desolate;
No fate seemed fair as mine,
No happiness so great!

And Nature, day by day,
Has sung in accents clear
This joyous roundelay,
"He loves thee – he is here.
Fal, la, la, la, Fal, la, la, la.
He loves thee – he is here.
Fal, la, la, Fal, la!"

~ Sir William S. Gilbert, 1879

Chapter 26

SEX MEANS MORE THAN YOU REALIZE

Let him kiss me with the kisses of his mouth –
for your love is more delightful than wine.
~ Song of Solomon 1:2

Making Love is the deepest, most intimate Communication between a husband and wife. It reunites them in a way that happens wity no other. Becoming One Flesh is Beautiful.

Woman is perhaps God's greatest invention. He created her specifically to meet the relational, emotional, and physical needs of His first invention: Man. He designed her in such a way that man was automatically drawn to her in wonder … she joyously gave herself to him … and both enjoyed Joyous Rapture that could have been everlasting.

But through sin and shame, the beauty of the male-female relationship became tarnished, convoluted, mixed up, and messed up. Instead of rejoicing in our differences, we are afraid of losing ourselves to the other. In our fear, we hide.

Or we seek to control and change one another to be more like ourselves … as though we were God Himself and, therefore, mindful of the only "right" way of being, which always backfires with serious and detrimental results.

Throughout history, we see examples of the exploitation of God's creation. We see woman used and abused by man, diminished in importance by his use of her for his pleasure and power. Man is also abused by woman, diminished in importance by her use of him. There are documented cases of women being mistreated, but men are also mistreated and abused … and in more ways than we can ever imagine.

Why Woman?

Men need women. And they have from the very beginning. It wasn't man's idea. Adam was clueless about what he was missing in the Garden. But the Lord knew he would need a woman to love and to adore. And to soften him. Otherwise, he would become domineering and consumed by his power.

In His infinite wisdom, the Creator designed a woman who would possess something inherently fascinating that would make her utterly irresistible to her husband. And it's not just about sex. Men desire women at a very deep level.

But too many women believe men are only interested in sex. Yes, they are interested in sex. Sex is very important to him. It meets an important need, but it's not all that he needs.

That said, making love to his wife fulfills many, many more of a man's needs than any other single thing his wife does for him. Making Love to his wife will naturally fulfill his needs for her attention, affection, acceptance, appreciation, and admiration. But that's not all …

Making Love makes a man feel … *loved!*

Sadly enough, too many men have given up on being loved by a woman, which is one of man's deepest longings. They have resigned themselves to settling for a measure of peace, giving up their hope for the fullness of a Joyous Marriage.

And that's sad. Very, very sad.

Do women like sex? Or only the Romance?

You've no doubt heard some very discouraging info about the long-term viability of Romance. For far too long, we've blindly taken the advice of far too many well-educated and well-meaning, but sadly-misinformed-and-pessimistic folks. It's time to learn the Truth about the inherent need of man for woman – and woman's need for man!

In brief, psychology and Christianity have both been telling us that Romance simply doesn't last. It simply can't because no one can stay on a romantic "high" forever. Romance is a "trick" of Mother Nature (our biology) designed to facilitate our attraction to one another and to compel us to mate.

When I was teaching at the university a few years ago, my department chair forwarded a student email message to me. She was looking for a prof who would be willing to assist with her research project about the harmfulness of romantic movies. Where she got that idea was an easy enough guess. Not long ago, my own pastor preached on how Hollywood sets up unrealistic expectations for relationships.

Our expectations are too high?

Our lack of Romantic success suggests that our expectations are too low! Why? Because we will always behave in ways that are consistent with our core beliefs. So I replied to my department chair that I would be very happy to speak with the student about romantic movies, but that I would not be giving her the response she was seeking. And for the first time, I was tempted to write to my pastor!

Romantic movies – the truly romantic ones, not the sexually inappropriate stuff – tap into the deepest desires of both men and women to enjoy a lasting emotionally intimate connection with another. And we've got the very best and blessed opportunity to enjoy that connection in the context of Marriage … if only we'd realize God's intention for us.

I believe professional counselor Tim Alan Gardner is correct in his approach:

> A couple's sexual relationship has a far higher purpose than pleasure or procreation. Scripture makes it clear that sex is the one thing on earth that joins two people into one. Now readers can learn how to approach marital sex in a way that brings the fulfillment of true oneness. *Sacred Sex* shows how they can experience a beautiful, God-ordained life of intimacy that blesses them far beyond the bedroom walls, serves as an act of worship to God, and touches their hearts and souls in ways they never could have imagined. (Amazon Book Description)

Sex without Romance is empty.

Men need to protect the sexuality of all women, not take it from them. That's true even after marriage! Men, you all want your wife to want to give herself to you willingly and affectionately. You never want to beg or bargain for sex.

Sex and affection are critical components of the marital relationship. Do you and your mate (or soon-to-be-mate) talk openly about your physical desire for one another? If you're engaged to be married, how have you chosen to deal with your increasing desire for one another? God Himself designed us so that our physical desire will grow naturally even as our love and commitment to one another grow.

The Marvelously Magnificent Marriage of Companionship, Commitment, Romance, and Sex ... a Divine Experience! So reconnect often, enjoy Fun and Friendship, then fan the flames of Passion to keep your Romance alive.

Gentlemen: Touch your lady often. Don't make it sexual. Make it Romantic. For example, look into her eyes, take her hand in yours, lift it slowly to your lips, and kiss it softly. Gently lower her hand while looking sweetly into her eyes. Smile, turn, and walk away slowly. What a total turn on!

All Expressions of Affection Count!

There's nothing more calming than making contact with the person you love most. So make physical contact as often as you can. You don't have to be dramatic about it. Start slow, guys. Ladies, his brain will notice even if he doesn't.

A Note to the Ladies About Cuddling: If it puts him in the mood for sex, take it as a positive indicator that he's a normal male. God created man in such a way that when he's close to the woman he loves, he gets aroused and wants to make love to her. How cool is that?

And while I'm on the subject … when a godly man makes love to his wife, he meets her emotional needs, as well her physical needs. You do remember Eve's passion for Adam? Women love sex, too. As a man approaches his wife from the holy place of love and understanding, he has the unique ability to make her feel loved, cherished and very desirable, especially as he respects her tender emotions.

Tender Moments

Tender moments require your awareness of one another. But most of us go through life in "task mode" instead of "people mode." Women are prone to do this, especially if they have small children. And men are prone to do this when they're overly focused on their careers. So it's no wonder so many men and women feel disconnected from their mates … and unloved … at the end of the day.

When did you last take the time to notice one another – to actually *see* your mate – as you go about your daily routine?

Research shows that most women continue to take primary responsibility for the home and children, even when they are working full time outside the home. And multitasking can be exhausting. Remember, long before that term was coined, we called *multitaskers* by another name: Moms.

Gentlemen: If your wife works outside the home, ask her what you can do to make her life a little smoother in the evenings. Dishes? Walking the dog? Bathing the kids? Folding laundry? Then resolve to do at least one thing every night ... that she knows she can always count on. As a Gift (i.e., without expectations) to the woman you love!

And, yes, that is sexy. Very romantic and very sexy.

Sometimes, it's the girl who's got it wrong.

Many people believe relationships go sideways because the guy screwed something up. That's not always the case.

Women make a lot of assumptions ... filling in "the blanks" with thoughts that paint a negative picture. We usually do it because we're afraid in the beginning ... afraid that something will go wrong. So we're almost relieved when it does. Then we can blame the guy. How wrong is that?

Couples always get back together at the end of the movie ... dancing cheek-to-cheek and pants-to-pants. So do couples who are having trouble ... when they learn to listen to one another and find out what's really going on.

Let him know how important he is: Make love to him!

A woman is frequently surprised if she hears that her man feels like he's simply not that important to her ... that he doesn't believe he's very high on her list of priorities. In fact, he might feel like he's not even *on* her list!

He may believe that he's nothing more than a paycheck to her ... something to be used up by her. And he doesn't want sex in exchange for his paycheck. He honestly wants to feel emotionally *connected* to her, but he just can't figure out how to make it happen. You can help with that, yes?

BONUS: Research shows that making love to your mate is a great way to immediately lessen stress!

Part 7

Submission in the 21st Century

AN OLD-FASHIONED IDEA

Our culture – with the well-intentioned assistance of more than a few overly zealous feminists – has all but obliterated God's plan for a man and a woman.

Some Christians totally ignore the concept of submission, whereas others read Paul's words as permission for husbands to dominate and/or abuse their wives.

Neither option, of course, is acceptable, and neither will create the loving and romantic relationship you desire.

My approach to healthy relationships is often labeled as an old-fashioned, out-dated notion about Love and Marriage.

Some have suggested it's rooted in the 1950s.

Or in the Victorian Era.

But it's much older.

In fact, it's Ancient.

Chapter 27

THE BEAUTY OF THE FEMININE

Now as the church submits to Christ,
so also wives should submit to their husbands in everything.
~ Ephesians 5: 24

I've always thought that if woman was created for man, and if what we're doing for him isn't working, then we probably should be spending some serious time finding out what it is we were intended to do for him!

To put it quite simply, I believe all we need to do is show up – to be fully present, available, and responsive to him. That is, we get to enjoy being the girl – and let him enjoy it, too! But not passive in the process! Au contraire, mon cher!

Woman: A Personal Gift from Heaven

When God created Adam, He knew one person wouldn't enough to fulfill His dreams. Although, Adam was clueless about what he was missing, his All-Wise Creator wasn't. The Lord knew man could not do so very well on his own. He would need someone to adore. So God's personal gift to Adam was his woman – created from his own body. So much like himself, yet so very different, Eve would have the natural capacity to complete Adam and to help focus his passion on someone outside of himself.

In the 21st Century, a man's longing for love is intended to spur him into the realization that his wife is God's gift to him – his reason for living – his hope and his joy in the full experience of the Lord's goodness. And most men get that. Honestly they do. Without a godly wife, a man will starve to death emotionally and relationally. Instead, with her by his side, he gets to feast on her femininity – to draw energy and inspiration from the closeness of her Beauty.

Feminine Strength + Submission = Beauty

Do you consider yourself a strong woman? Many of us do. But what is the Source of your strength? By now, you'd think I'd know myself pretty well, and I do. Yet I'm amazed at how the Lord continually reveals truth to me ... not only about others, but also about myself.

I knew I was pretty good at that "submission" stuff in my first marriage, but I didn't realize until recently, that I didn't understand the whole equation. My submission wasn't by choice. It was rooted in my fear. Fear of displeasing my husband ... and losing him. And because of my fear, I was never a truly strong woman. And I lost my husband.

Many women I meet are good at that "strength" stuff in their marriages. But is their strength also rooted in fear?

Sometimes we toughen ourselves up to get through life, and we lose our true strength in the process. In other words, many women develop a false sense of strength as a defense against being hurt. But in the end, it causes them and their partners to experience unnecessary pain, and they both lose.

Defensiveness simply doesn't work in marriage. Ever.

So what's the source of our True Strength? It's the Joy of the Lord. He is Our Strength and Our Song. We abide in Him, and He produces the Fruits of the Spirit within us. Truly, there's nothing sweeter than that!

So learn to live in the reality that the Lord cherishes you as His Beloved Daughter. And that His desire is to teach your husband to cherish you, too!

Submission must be a choice.

From True Strength you have the wonderful opportunity to *choose* Submission ... to the Lord first, then to your husband. That's what makes a woman truly Beautiful.

Clearly, we are created as partners. Essential partners in the work of the Kingdom of God. Through Christ, we are redeemed to fulfill the purpose for which we were created. Man is the Leader, and woman is the Follower. He's not a dictator, and she's not a silent, powerless subject.

Fortunately, as we get things back in their proper, Heavenly perspective, man has what he needs to do his job, to live out his life passionately doing what God designed him to do.

As a wife, you are created to be your husband's "rescuer" (Genesis 2), so it's important to know exactly how to do that ... and how to do it really well. So much of your husband's success depends on your walk with the Lord ... and your desire to be the woman that he needs you to be.

As women, we have never been without the relationship of another human being. We, therefore conclude that we are the "Relationship Experts."

But most of us make the grievous error of believing it is our job ... as the "Relationship Expert" ... to fix, manage, and control a man. Indeed, it is most assuredly not! We have a much Higher Purpose!

A woman has been given to her mate as Sweet Companion and Confidant. He is motivated simply by her presence, and he will do almost anything to make her smile.

She's there to let him know when he's on the right track, not to criticize him when he's not. Her positive, affirming influence will cause her man to excel and, most importantly, to grow in his relationship with The Lord.

What if she doesn't think he's on the right track?

You remember what we talked about in Chapter 22, right? A godly woman will always pray first, then expresses her concern lovingly (Ephesians 4:15) ... and briefly. She may be assured that he heard her the first time. So her job from that moment forward is to pray for her mate with insight, fully confident that The Lord will answer her prayers.

If her man needs changing, The Lord will most surely do it (1 John 5:14). However, she must remain humble, knowing that it also might be *her* that The Lord desires to change.

How to Help a Man Take Leadership

First, he needs to know that you are following him, even if he's not a very seasoned leader. A man can never become a really great leader if no one is willing to follow him. In a word, he needs you to submit to his leadership. Submission really means that you trust and respect him. It does not mean that you follow him blindly and mindlessly.

Second, he really needs your feedback. Both Scripture and research show that men need to be open to the influence of their wives. Otherwise, they're doomed to fail.

However, your feedback mustn't be in the form of criticism, attack, blame, or advice. What he desperately needs to hear is when he is getting it right ... when he's doing something that pleases you ... that makes you happy. And remember he needs you to help him look good to anyone who's watching. He'll stand taller and work harder than you ever thought possible. Yes, just give him that, and he'll pull out all the stops to please you – more so than you ever imagined.

Chapter 28

THE PASSION OF THE MASCULINE

Husbands, love your wives, just as Christ loved
the church and gave himself up for her ....
~ Ephesians 5:25

For some time now, I have believed that we women have far more influence than we realize. Many words have been used to describe this phenomenon, but men cannot resist us. At least, not for very long.

Basically, when you understand what you mean to him and know how to fulfill your purpose in his life, any man with a reasonable amount of emotional health naturally responds with all the love and tenderness you desire from him.

Yes, in case you're wondering, most men are reasonably healthy. They just express it differently than we do. And isn't that what draws us to them in the first place? What we love so much about them? What we adore?

Inspiring the Adventurer

Without a doubt, a wife's decision to submit to her husband doesn't get the best press in today's culture. Such a woman is thought to be a bit on the crazy side ... or not too bright. But nothing could be further from the Truth!

Yes, Scripture instructs a woman to live for her husband. But when you read the entirety of Ephesians 5, you realize she doesn't have the more difficult role. Her husband does ... because he must be willing to die for her!

The simple fact of the matter is that nothing inspires a godly man more than experiencing the Beauty of his wife. He's naturally drawn to her strength as she basks in the Joy of the Lord. His heart and soul are softened by the Fruits of the Spirit that flow out of her as a matter of fact.

And as she chooses to honor him as her leader – to submit to him out of trust and respect for who he is and for who he is becoming – the fullness of his Passion for life automatically propels him forward toward his destiny!

To fulfill his Purpose, a man needs to tap into his masculine Passion. And a wise woman knows how to build up her husband and thereby increase his Passion to fuel the Power he needs to Produce results.

Inspire or Usurp?

> *The wise woman builds her house,*
> *but with her own hands the foolish one tears hers down.*
> ~ Proverbs 14:1

Time to pause right here for a commercial break in the form of a definition or two. To *inspire* is to evoke an emotion that moves him to want to do something. To *usurp* is to take his power ... without the right to do so.

The first strategy builds up your man ... and your home. The second tears him down ... and your home.

I totally get how women get caught in this cycle! Remember *Chapter 14: Women and Anxiety*? If you don't, please go back there now because this is really, really important!

Anxious people try to achieve a sense of control and thereby reduce their anxiety. And we women are often anxious ... or worried ... about almost everything.

Sidebar ...

There's no doubt in my mind that – if this book were written by a man – the men reading this would get the impression they were doing everything wrong. Because guys are really hard on themselves – and each other!

But because I'm a woman ... and because Scripture tells us that we're here to help our man – it just makes more sense to focus on what she can do – not so much on what he can do – even though he can surely do an awful lot to make things a whole lot better, too.

For the guy's list, review *Part 4: The Beauty of a Woman*!

But honestly, ladies, you do have the following choices!

Feminine Strength (the Joy of the Lord)
+ Submission (by choice)
= Feminine Beauty (that inspires Masculine Passion)
or
Feminine Anxiety (a false strength based in fear)
+ Control (a defense against fear)
= Emasculation (that usurps Masculine Authority)

Men, make no mistake.

You are held responsible, no matter what your wife does. I'm only making the point here that when his wife tries to run things, give him advice, or "wear the pants," a man is drained of the Passion he needs to fulfill his Purpose.

Even so, the Holy Spirit is always with you. Do not resort to exerting your Power alone. Because Power without love is destructive ... for her and for you!

Without her inspiration, a husband can become a couch potato at best and a domineering cad at worst. In other words, he'll go to one or the other of extremes in regard to his God-given Masculine Power.

That is, he'll give up on life. "What's the point?" And no one will benefit from what he has to offer the world.

Or he'll become aggressive. And no one will win that game. Least of all, him.

Does this fit your guy? I don't know. Ask him!

Mostly, this is what I hear from the men I've spoken with. Especially from men who bring their wives to talk with me about their relationship.

Week after week, I watch men as they long for their wives to treat them with trust and respect. Most of the time, his wife doesn't even know how she's coming across to him.

I love to help them both with that. Because there they sit ... each feeling an intense longing to love and to be loved ... and not seeing the proverbial forest for the proverbial trees.

Even the Park Ranger Knows

Awhile back, Fred and I were dancing with friends at one of our favorite outdoor venues, when a park ranger appeared.

Although the ranger's intent was to inform us that the park had closed 37 minutes earlier, he was simply standing there watching us in awe. A dozen couples ranging in age from 30-something to 60-something, enjoying a pleasant summer evening engaged in an activity right from the 19th Century. Perhaps it was just our Victorian costumes that fascinated him, but I believe it was much more.

As Fred and the others loaded their cars to leave, I chatted with the ranger. "Fred and I offer workshops for couples.

We want men to know how it feels to have a woman follow them and make them feel good about their ability to lead. And we want women to know how wonderful it feels to be treated like a lady."

The ranger turned his head and looked at me in shock. "There are still women who want to follow a man?"

"Yes, they do. At least most Christian women do. In fact, they love it. And even long for it!"

Still in apparent disbelief, the ranger reported, "I read something the other day about most women making more money than men … and that most women believe they don't even need men around anymore."

"That's not true for all women. Not the good ones anyway." I replied confidently … because I know the Truth.

Our conversation ended there, but knowing a little about how a man's mind works, I'm pretty sure he continued to process the whole thing … seeing us there, watching the dance. Wondering what it would be like if he himself could find a woman who would trust and respect him.

And if that's even a remote possibility …

Sonnets from the Portuguese #43

How do I love thee? Let me count the ways.
I love thee to the depth and breadth and height
My soul can reach, when feeling out of sight
For the ends of Being and ideal Grace.
I love thee to the level of every day's
Most quiet need, by sun and candlelight.
I love thee freely, as men strive for Right;
I love thee purely, as they turn from Praise.
I love with a passion put to use
In my old griefs, and with my childhood's faith.
I love thee with a love I seemed to lose
With my lost saints, I love thee with the breath,
Smiles, tears, of all my life! And, if God choose,
I shall but love thee better after death.

~ Elizabeth Barrett Browning, 1845

Conclusion
The Perfect Partnership

BETTER THAN EDEN

"I will repay you for the years the locusts have eaten –
the great locust and the young locust,
the other locusts and the locust swarm –
my great army that I sent among you.

"You will have plenty to eat, until you are full,
and you will praise the name of the LORD your God,
who has worked wonders for you;
never again will my people be shamed.

"Then you will know that I am in Israel,
that I am the LORD your God,
and that there is no other;
never again will my people be shamed.

"And afterward,
I will pour out my Spirit on all people.
Your sons and daughters will prophesy,
your old men will dream dreams,
your young men will see visions.

"Even on my servants, both men and women,
I will pour out my Spirit in those days."

~ Joel 2:25-29

A Self-Fulfilling Prophecy

If you're in a not-so-good place right now, you've got plenty of company. Many of us have been where you are at one time or another – myself included. The Truth is that we always end up where we are because of what we believe ... about ourselves and our mates ... or future mates.

Most of us act as though we're still living under the curse. Is it any wonder that women continue to try to fix, manage, and control their husbands, and that men resist their wives' efforts and attempt to establish their identity in their work?

Many couples spend the bigger part of their days imagining the worst about one another. Then they're surprised when their evening doesn't go well. How crazy is that?

And most counselors spend a lot of time rehashing what's wrong with one or partner or the other, believing that their analysis will produce the magic solution to unhappiness. It's like trying to get rid of a pink elephant by concentrating on how the pink elephant walks and talks and looks.

If it walks and talks and looks like a pink elephant, it must be a pink elephant. So if you want to be rid of it, you don't analyze it to death. You kick it out and put something better in its place ... like a tenderness and love for your mate.

Helping the Boy Win Back His Girl

A friend once commented, "I don't know how you can sit and listen to couples argue all the time, day after day."

"I don't," I said. "If all I did was listen to arguments, I'd be severely depressed. So I just help the boy win back his girl."

Most happy, healthy couples don't go to counseling, though some do. But mostly I see people who are in pain. Which means I get to participate in the Lord's redemptive work.

Confidence and Hope

I remain confident of this: I will see the goodness
of the Lord in the land of the living.
~ Psalm 27:13

I couldn't do this work without hope ... and the realization that God is in everything I do. He's the one Who does the healing and growing. But I get to help, and it's Wonderful!

The Truth is ... whether you are male or female, you were creatively designed for Romance, and the Lord is deeply interested, not only in your Holiness, but also in the depth of your Happiness. After all, Joy is a fruit of the Spirit!

He's always there for you to enjoy, and He wants you to enjoy one another, too! If He created the whole idea of Marriage, then He must be invested in seeing Love come to fruition in your life. For your pleasure, but also as a light to show the world just how very much He loves us all!

Conversations With God

The Lord doesn't want us to wander aimlessly through Life, making mistake after mistake. So He talks with us. We only need to train our ears to hear Him.

"The one who enters by the gate is the shepherd of the sheep.
The gatekeeper opens the gate for him, and the sheep listen to his
voice. He calls his own sheep by name and leads them out.
When he has brought out all his own, he goes on ahead of them,
and his sheep follow him because they know his voice."
~ John 10:2-4

When I first meet a couple, I don't know the details of their next Chapter. But I know it's beginning for them. If they can only imagine it, it's going to be amazing.

Because whenever the Lord puts His hand to something, it's always more than we could ever hope, ask, or imagine ....

And you must realize by now ... my hope is high, I ask a lot ... and I have a really, really Romantic Imagination.

She: What are you showing me through this part of my journey, Papa? My back-roads drive to Palm Springs comes to mind. The scenery changed – my viewpoint changed so many times in just a few hours. Then there was that huge mountain. I didn't even know it was there – because of my viewpoint.

Papa: There are many things you cannot see now, but they are there. That is true for him, too. And that's why your focus must be on Me. I know what lies ahead, and My Spirit is guiding you both. You are taking different paths, and you will both arrive on schedule.

She: Thank you for keeping me from shame. I know that where I am isn't my destination, and I long to arrive!

Papa: You are in a desert place, but I will make streams for you in the desert. I'm here with you. Just keep writing. You will look back on this time and see My purpose.

She: I feel pressure to make this good. It seems ordinary to me. Nothing special. Nothing world-changing.

Papa: Really? That's not how I see it.

She: Why the return to painful longing?

Papa: Because you know of the joy that is before you. You have tasted it, and it is good. Longing is part of the journey. Yes, you will be satisfied. Deeply satisfied. And your hunger will return – only to be satisfied again and again.

Keep Me in view in all things.
And I will give you the desires of your heart.

Now to him who is able to do
immeasurably more than all we ask or imagine,
according to his power that is at work within us,
to him be glory in the church
and in Christ Jesus throughout all generations,
for ever and ever! Amen.
~Ephesians 3:20-21

And They Lived Happily Ever After

She stands alone on the veranda ... her gaze fixed on the clearness of the lake below as she recalls the path of her own Love Story.

So far, it's been filled with delightful twists and distressing turns, as well as fabulous twirls of astonishment. And she's traveled very far from the sewage of her earlier chapters. Surrounded only by beauty now.

She hears the door open and the soft sound of his footsteps, but she doesn't turn to look. She knows who's behind her.

Her husband slips his strong arms tenderly around her waist. With a gentle kiss to the top of her head, he simply whispers, "I love you."

They stand silently for a long time, savoring the moment. Soon everything will spring to life in preparation for the impending arrival of weekend guests. God is so good.

Her Handsome King turns her around, and looks into her eyes with obvious pleasure. She sparkles back at him.

After few moments of soft kisses, they enter their private residence to prepare breakfast together. Holding hands as they enjoy one last cup of coffee before the day officially begins, he reads Scripture aloud to her ... as he always does.

Today he reads Psalm 16:5-8.

Lord, you alone are my portion and my cup;
you make my lot secure.

The boundary lines have fallen for me in pleasant places;
surely I have a delightful inheritance.

I will praise the Lord, who counsels me;
even at night my heart instructs me.

I keep my eyes always on the Lord.
With him at my right hand, I will not be shaken.

Tears of joy fill her eyes.

And as he prays aloud, tears of joy fill both their eyes. They realize how very blessed they are to have the Lord as the Author of their Love Story.

Their secret? They know who they are and Whose they are. Created in His image, they were sinners saved by His grace. And now they're called to be Saints.

The Lord doesn't come down each day to walk with them in their Paradise … because He is residing inside each of them.

Theirs is now a Perfect Partnership with the Lord. United in Christ, they demonstrate the oneness He created for a man and a woman both to enjoy …

… a oneness that's Better Than Eden.

When We All Get to Heaven

Sing the wondrous love of Jesus,
Sing His mercy and His grace;
In the mansions bright and blessed
He'll prepare for us a place.

When we all get to heaven,
What a day of rejoicing that will be!
When we all see Jesus,
We'll sing and shout the victory!

While we walk the pilgrim pathway,
Clouds will overspread the sky;
But when trav'ling days are over,
Not a shadow, not a sigh.

Let us then be true and faithful,
Trusting, serving every day;
Just one glimpse of Him in glory
Will the toils of life repay.

Onward to the prize before us!
Soon His beauty we'll behold;
Soon the pearly gates will open;
We shall tread the streets of gold.

Eliza E. Hewitt, 1898

Bibliography

Ainsworth, M., Blehar, M. Waters, E., & Wall, S. (1978). *Patterns of attachment: A psychological study of the Strange Situation.* Hillsdale, NJ: Lawrence Erlbaum Associates.

Allender, D. B., & Longman, T. (1995). *Intimate allies: Rediscovering God's design for marriage and becoming soul mates for life.* Wheaton, IL: Tyndale House Publishers, Inc.

Bartholomew, K., & Horowitz, L. M. (1991). Attachment styles among young adults: A test of a four-category model. *Journal of Personality and Social Psychology, 61,* 226-244.

Bergman, S. J. (1995). Men's psychological development: A relational perspective. In R. F. Levant & W. S. Pollack (Eds.), *A new psychology of men* (pp. 68-90). New York: Basic Books.

Bowlby, J. (1979). *The making and breaking of affectional bonds.* New York: Methuen.

Brody, L. R. (1993). On understanding gender differences in the expression of emotion: Gender roles, socialization, and language. In S. L. Ablon, D. Brown, E. J. Khantzian, & J. E. Mack (Eds.), *Human feelings: Explorations in affect development and meaning* (pp. 87-121). Hillsdale, NJ: Analytic Press.

Brody, L. R. (1997). Gender and emotion: Beyond stereotypes. *Journal of Social Issues, 53,* 369-394. Retrieved May 18, 2002, from ProQuest Research Library database.

Brody, L. R. (2000). The socialization of gender differences in emotional expression: Display rules, infant temperament, and differentiation. In A. H. Fischer (Ed.), *Gender and emotion: Social psychological perspectives* (pp. 24-47). New York: Cambridge University Press.

Brody, L. R., & Hall, J. A. (1993). Gender and emotion. In M. Lewis & J. M. Haviland (Eds.), *Handbook of emotions* (pp. 447-460). New York: Guilford Press.

Catt, M. C., Hemmings, T., & McBride, J. (Producers), & Kendrick, A. (Director). (2008). *Fireproof* [Motion picture]. United States of America: Sherwood Pictures.

Catt, M. C., Hemmings, T., & McBride, J. (Producers), & Kendrick, A. (Director). (2011). *Courageous* [Motion picture]. United States of America: Sherwood Pictures.

Cooke, G. (2007). *Permission granted* [Audio CD]. Vancouver, WA: Brilliant Book House.

Eldredge, J. (2011). *Wild at heart revised and updated: Discovering the secret of a man's soul.* Nashville, TN: Thomas Nelson Publishers.

Erre, M. (2011). *Marriage* [Podcast]. Irvine, CA: Mariners Church. http://www.drdebismith.com/ephesians_5.html

Gardner, T. A. (2002). *Sacred sex: A spiritual celebration of oneness in marriage paperback.* Colorado Springs, CO: WaterBrook Press.

Gottman, J. (1999). *The seven principles for making marriage work.* New York: Crown Publishing Group.

Greenson, R. R. (1968). Dis-identifying from mother: Its special importance for the boy. *International Journal of Psycho-Analysis, 49,* 370-374.

Gurian, M. (1994). *Mothers, sons, and lovers: How a man's relationship with his mother affects the rest of his life.* Boston: Shambhala Publications, Inc.

Gurian, M. (1996). *The wonder of boys: What parents, mentors, and educators can do to shape boys into exceptional men.* New York: Jeremy P. Tarcher/Putnam.

Hazan, C., & Shaver, P. (1987). Romantic love conceptualized as an attachment process. *Journal of Personality and Social Psychology, 52,* 511-524.

Johnson, B. (Producer), & Crowe, D. (Director). (1996). *Jerry Maguire* [Motion picture]. United States of America: Sony/Columbia.

Johnson, S. (2008). *Hold me tight: Seven conversations for a lifetime of love.* New York: Little, Brown, and Company.

Karen, R. (1998). *Becoming attached: First relationships and how they shape our capacity to love.* New York: Oxford University Press.

Levinson, D. J. (1986). *The seasons of a man's life.* New York: Ballentine Books.

Locke, H. J., & Wallace, K. M. (1959). Short marital-adjustment and prediction tests: Their reliability and validity. *Marriage and Family Living, 21,* pp. 251-255.

MacDonald, G. (1996). *When men think private thoughts: Exploring issues that captivate the minds of men.* Nashville, TN: Thomas Nelson Publishers.

Morris, G. (2012). *Men: The simpler sex?* Retrieved September 15, 2012, from http://www.net-burst.net/love/men.htm

Penner, C. L., & Penner, J. J. (1994). *Getting your sex life off to a great start: A guide for engaged and newlywed couples.* Nashville, TN: Thomas Nelson

Pollack, S. (Producer), & Lee, A. (Director). (1995). *Sense and sensibility* [Motion picture]. United States of America: Columbia Pictures.

Pollack, W. S. (1998). *Real boys: Rescuing our sons form the myths of boyhood.* New York: Henry Holt and Company.

Rhodes, R. (1997). How did Lucifer fall and become Satan? Retrieved March 29, 2014, from http://www.christianity.com/theology/theological-faq/how-did-lucifer-fall-and-become-satan-11557519.html

Rhodes, R. (2013). *The debate over feminist theology: Which view is biblical?* Retrieved March 29, 2014, from http://www.ronrhodes.addr.com/articles/the-debate-over-feminist.html

Salkind, I. (Producer), & Donner, R. (Director). (1978). *Superman: The movie* [Motion picture]. United States of America: Warner Bros.

Smith, D. L. (2009). *Mothers and sons: How the maternal attachment experience affects boys' emotional and social development.* Garden Grove, CA: OC Christian Counseling.

Smith, D. L. (2009). *Why won't he talk to me? The simple truth about men and intimate communication.* Garden Grove, CA: OC Christian Counseling.

Dr. Debi was able to help us realize that we,
my husband (a male) and I (a female), are different. DUH!

She helped me see that I had expectations for my husband
based on my own expectations for myself.

I expected my husband, who is mentally wired differently,
raised differently, processes differently, communicates
differently and is even biologically built differently, to act
like me, a female.

Once I was able to realize those differences, I was able to
listen and learn what HE needed from me instead of what I
thought he needed.

This new outlook opened up new conversations which have
led to a level of depth that neither of us knew existed.

We are extremely grateful to Dr. Debi for showing us the
tools we need to love each other, respect each other, and
take care of each other in the way that Christ intended us to.

~ Emily

Dear Dr. Debi,

I thank God for leading us to you and your sincere, knowledgeable and anointed spirit and teaching!

From you, we've each learned a lot about each other, about communication, and in better understanding each others' emotions.

More importantly, I believe your teaching (and your "person") has been instrumental in each of us strengthening our relationships with God (most importantly, my Husband's).

We cannot be thankful enough for you saving our marriage (would seem almost impossible to most), and also to restoring it to much better than before the separation!

We love you.

~ CM

Dr. Debi Smith is passionate about helping Christian couples and single adults apply biblical principles and the findings of scientific research to everyday life.

She earned her Doctorate in Clinical Psychology (PsyD), with a Minor in Applied Theology, from Rosemead School of Psychology at Biola University.

As a Licensed Psychologist, Dr. Debi has studied the Psychology of Men and Traditional Masculinity at both graduate and post-doctoral levels, and has even taught a university class on this very popular subject.

She's learned that most marriage counseling ignores Scripture, research, or both. She uses research to explain the *how* and *why* of Scripture. She believes that God Himself has a Plan for Romance and Marriage based on His Love. And that's her Message.

She's also learned that most women don't have a clue about men's experience, and that most men don't know how to explain it. And that's her Mission.

Connect With Dr. Debi Online:

www.DrDebiSmith.com
Twitter.com/DrDebiSmith
Facebook.com/OCChristianCounseling
YouTube.com/user/DrDebiSmith
www.OCChristianCounseling.com
www.OCChristianCouples.com